To Mary

A token of our love
and in remembrance
of our historic
family occasion at
"Valetta" 29th Aug '89
when you + Frank
came all the way from
Patricks Point
Brendan, Johanna
myles, Kielan Rossa
and Hanna.

Irish Standard Gauge Railways

Tom Middlemass

DAVID & CHARLES
Newton Abbot   London   North Pomfret (Vt)

British Library Cataloguing in Publication Data

Middlemass, Tom
  Irish standard gauge railways.
  1. Railroads – Ireland – History
  I. Title
  385'.09413   H63048   80–41447

  ISBN 0–7153–8007–9

Photoset by
Northern Phototypesetting Co Bolton
Printed in Great Britain
by Biddles Ltd, Guildford, Surrey
for David & Charles (Publishers) Limited
Brunel House, Newton Abbot, Devon

Published in the United States of America
by David & Charles Inc
North Pomfret, Vermont 05053, USA

Contents

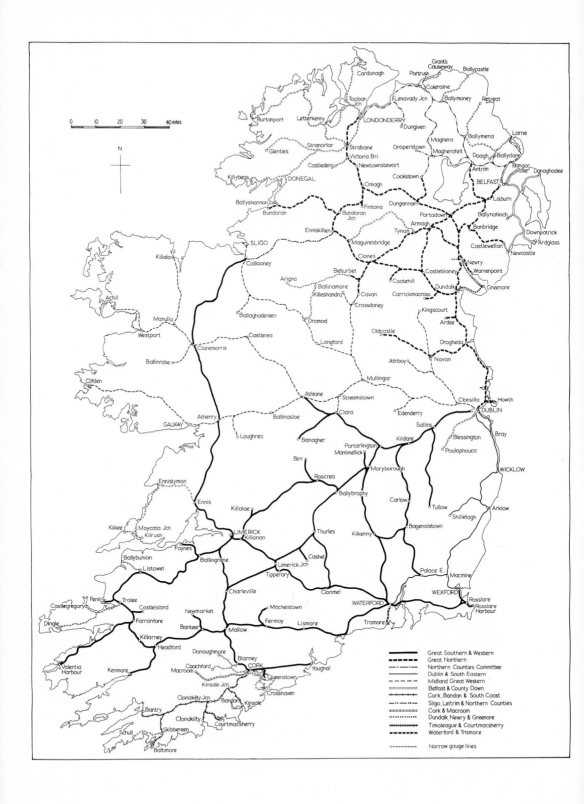

PREFACE

The fact that Ireland existed for a hundred years and more as a constituent member of the United Kingdom had curiously little beneficial effect on the development of its railway system. In 1831 its $7\frac{3}{4}$ million population was as eager as the remaining two-thirds of the UK to welcome the Railway Age, yet, for a variety of reasons, progress in Ireland was abominably slow. One cannot avoid the conclusion that much of this lethargy emanated from Westminster where, all through the 19th century, a succession of British Governments proved themselves uniformly unimaginative in assessing Irish needs. The House of Lords was particularly obstructive.

In 1836 a Royal Commission set up to examine Irish railway prospects took two years to conclude that, as railways in Ireland were never likely to prove remunerative, construction of two main lines – one to the north, one to the south – would suffice. A rider was added that if no private company could be found to undertake these tasks state assistance should be provided. Though Irish reaction was overwhelmingly favourable, the British government exhibited little enthusiasm, and a tentative scheme eventually piloted through the House of Commons was smothered in the Lords. In the event state aid amounting to $£2\frac{1}{2}$ millions did emerge, but so did renewed political conviction that prime responsibility rested still upon the reluctant shoulders of private enterprise. The effect of this upon Ireland is forcibly chronicled by Disraeli in his *Life of Lord George Bentinck* (1852):

In 1846 Acts of Parliament were in existence authorising construction of 1,500 miles of railway in Ireland, and some of these Acts had passed as long as eleven years previously; yet at the end of 1846 only 123 miles of railway had been completed, and only 164 were in course of completion, though arrested in their progress for want of funds . . . The cause of weakness in Ireland to prosecute these undertakings was the total want of domestic capital for the purpose, and the unwillingness of English capitalists to embark their funds in a country whose social and political position they viewed with distrust.

One might add in this context a comment made by Gladstone when in 1844 he was sponsoring a Bill advocating revision of railway charges and Government purchase of Irish railways. He was replying to arguments of 'free enterprisers' in the House of Commons:

I would rather give my confidence to a Gracchus when speaking on the subject of sedition, than to a railway director when speaking to the public on the effect of competition.

Ironically, 20 years later Gladstone had the opportunity, as Prime Minister, to assist Irish railways, but retreated from the prospect.

Inherent handicaps or no, initial earning powers of Irish railways appreciated handsomely enough, until the Great Famine of 1847 arrived to inflict its grim toll of death and emigration. It was, in fact, at this critical juncture that Lord George Bentinck came forward with sweeping proposals to assist Irish railways by state loans. £16 million was demanded – once again, infinitely more modest measures won the day. A second Commission, appointed in 1865, contrived to squash such hopes as existed of effecting amalgamations amongst Ireland's over-numerous small railway concerns, now 17 in number. A minority report by one of its members, William Monsell MP, invoked the following comparison: 'The LNWR, in England, with a single Board earned an income of £5,300,000 on 1,200 miles of track. Irish railways, with many Boards, earned £1,520,000 on 1,700 miles.' Sir Rowland Hill, supporting him on principle, advocated gradual purchase of Irish railways by the state. Again, no action was taken.

The number of Irish companies continued to multiply – by 1868 it had risen to 39 – so, too, did agitation by Irish MPs in favour of State intervention. In 1869 Gladstone's government promised the matter 'careful attention'. After this sentiment was repeated in 1871 and 1873 Lord Claud Hamilton, with the whole of Ireland behind him, moved a motion in favour of State purchase, and lost. A further Royal Commission (1876), while conceding that Irish fares and working expenses were too high, still ruled against state purchase. A subsequent Select Committee of 1882 strongly advocated railway amalgamations in Ireland to reduce overheads, but by now such companies as GNR(I) were already taking their own initiative. The Railways and Canals Act of 1888 had many recommendations to offer, but litigation to be risked under its aegis was much too expensive a prospect for Ireland's impoverished railways to face. Thus the Act had little effect. One last political fling surfaced in 1906, when after repeated requests a Vice-Regal Commission was appointed. This time a majority report plumped for unification of Irish railways. A minority report stopped short at amalgamations, and again Westminster refrained from taking action of any sort. Then the Great War erupted, and the rules of the game were altered with fateful permanence, as we shall see.

Irish Standard Gauge
Immediately war broke out in 1914 all railways in England, Scotland and Wales were placed under command of a Railway Executive Committee. Irish railways, however, did not come under government control until 31 December 1916, and even then their rolling stock could not be commandeered for service abroad, for the Irish standard gauge was 5ft 3in. The story of how this came about provides one more example of the detached, almost colonial, manner in which Irish railways were viewed within the framework of the United Kingdom.

The first Irish railway to be formed was the Limerick & Waterford (incorporated 1826). As the line was never built, the distinction of operating Ireland's first railway fell to the Dublin & Kingstown (1831). Kingstown, formerly known as Dunleary, acquired its name when King George IV visited Ireland in 1821, but in recent times has been re-named Dun Laoghaire. Six miles from Dublin, it offered a convenient focal point for the wave of ambition which had been triggered-off in Ireland by the coming of the Railway Age. The line was opened on 17 December 1834, and following British practice, it was laid to a gauge of 4ft 8½in. So, too, was an odd extension of 1½ miles to Dalkey, opened seven years later. On this occasion atmospheric principles, as patented by Clegg and Samuda, were employed. Atmospheric trains ran uphill to Dalkey, and returned to Kingstown by gravity. In the event this was the first, and last, use of British standard gauge in Ireland, for a

Drummond Commission on Railway Communications in Ireland, appointed by Westminster in 1836, recommended adoption of 6ft 2in gauge for the whole of Ireland. The Ulster Railway, opening in 1839, duly implemented the Commission's proposals.

A year or two later the Dublin & Drogheda, working at the other end of the Dublin–Belfast route, outraged the Ulster by proposing to adopt a gauge of 5ft 2in. Appeal was made to the Board of Trade, opinions were taken from many engineers, and a final, somewhat bumbling, compromise of 5ft 3in emerged. This was accepted by Dublin & Drogheda, the Gauges (Ireland) Act of 1846 confirmed it was standard practice for all time to come, and the Ulster Railway tracks were altered accordingly in 1849. Compensation of £13,742 awarded the Ulster Railway was levied on adjoining railways which 'would stand to benefit by the change, and the consequent possibility of through running.'

Conclusions
In summarising the difficulties which beset the progress of Irish railways, one cannot ignore the traditionally unhelpful attitudes of British governments. Even after Partition in 1921, when both Irish governments set up independent commissions, inconsistency remained the order of the day. The Northern Ireland Commission favoured leaving railways as they were, while that of the Irish Free State proposed nationalisation, with separate board of control.

At one time it was fashionable to compare high rates and bad management of Irish railways unfavourably with their equivalents in other European countries, notably Belgium and the UK. Such criticisms tended to ignore difficulties which were almost unique to Ireland:
(1) The famine of 1847 decimated Ireland's population, thereby reducing potential passenger traffic at the very time when its railways were bound to expand.
(2) In any case Ireland's population was badly distributed from a railway point of view. Only 1¼ million of her citizens lived in cities or towns with populations of 5,000 or more; the bulk of these towns were already served by river or sea transport. Sea shipping eliminated a deal of railway freight traffic, while passenger traffic inland was thinly spread.
(3) Mineral resources in Ireland were insignificant, and what industry there was

tended to concentrate around ports. Fishing and agricultural industries were never highly enough developed to benefit railways to any great extent.

(4) Until 1921 all legislation passed by Westminster favoured English manufacturers. No Irish preferences were given, nor was there a tribunal in Ireland whereby traders could lodge complaints. Largely as a result, the density of railway traffic in England was seven times greater than in Ireland, while the later growth of motor transport hit Irish railways more severely, particularly during the 'Troubles'.

(5) The scattered nature of the Irish population meant that many small stations which were uneconomic were kept open. Staff reductions were so difficult to effect that even by 1926 Irish railways were employing over 19,000 men to service 3,400 route miles.

(6) If domestic locomotive construction at the GS&WR Inchicore workshops is omitted from the total, the proportion of remaining locomotives which owe their origin to British manufacture assumes colonial dimensions.

These difficulties, and others of like nature, constantly emerge as one proceeds to examine Irish railways on an individual company basis.

Finally a few words are necessary to unravel complications of station names, for during the 1960s CIE renamed a number of major stations after Irish patriots, the changes being shown below. Other stations in the Republic have changed from English to Irish renderings and some have bilingual signs not only for station names but also for station notices.

Former name (pre 1966)	*Present name*
Cork Glanmire Road	Cork Kent
Drogheda	Drogheda McBride
Dublin	Dublin
Amiens Street	Connolly
Kingsbridge	Heuston
Westland Row	Pearse
Dundalk	Dundalk Clarke
Limerick	Limerick Colbert
Tralee	Tralee Casement
Waterford North	Waterford Plunkett

Many stations on CIE have bilingual signs either for station names themselves or for general station notices. This was the sign at Mallow in the 1950s before the closure of the line to Fermoy and Waterford, and the Kenmare and Valentia Harbour branches.

CHAPTER ONE
DUBLIN & SOUTH EASTERN RAILWAY

Incorporated: 16 July 1846   *Opened:* 10 July 1854
Abosrbed by Great Southern Railways: 1 January 1925

When in an aura of great excitement Ireland's first railway was opened in 1834 its engineer, Charles Vignoles, envisaged eventual construction of a master line from Dublin to Valentia, where a great new port would arise to expedite travel between Europe and America. Far from realising this dream the Dublin & Kingstown only succeeded in forfeiting its own Dublin birthright once much more elementary propositions came its way via Paddington, London.

Glance at a map, and the relative positions of Wexford, Waterford and Fishguard explain immediately why the Great Western Railway in England was anxious to see the D&KR extend further south. Confronted with blunt proposals that the two Irish seaports should be linked to Dublin with the minimum of delay, D&KR management reacted rather warily. Subsequent discussions floundered-on with ever-decreasing conviction; the upshot was that in 1846 the Waterford, Wexford, Wicklow & Dublin Railway was launched in lieu. The GWR's continuing influence behind the scenes peeped out when the new company appointed as its first engineer one Isambard Kingdom Brunel. Later, perhaps the sheer audacity of employing the names of all four Irish south-west seaboard counties in the company's title occasioned blushes in the boardroom, for in 1848 WWW&DR's name was changed to the more modest one of Dublin & Wicklow.

Progress was not easy. The effects of the Great Famine did much to inhibit D&WR's construction plans. So, too, did protracted negotiations with a rival concern, the Dublin, Dundrum & Rathfarnham (1846). In 1851, the latter changed its name to Dublin & Bray, and conditions laid down in the same Act led to its absorption by D&WR two years later. A line to Bray was opened in 1854, and Wicklow was reached the following year. In 1855 Dublin & Kingstown metals, leased earlier to D&WR at £36,000 per annum, were re-gauged to 5ft 3in at a cost of £38,000; an additional £89,625 was spent converting the Kingstown–Dalkey atmospheric section to steam haulage.

The way was now clear for expansion, in terms urged by GWR a decade before. A further Act, obtained in 1860, authorised extension as far as Enniscorthy, while under the same aegis D&WR's title was altered to the more ambitious one of Dublin, Wicklow & Wexford Railway. Advance to Wexford, though achieved by August 1872, took longer than was anticipated. Access to Waterford was to prove an even more complex and time-consuming affair.

The key lay in territory controlled by Bagenalstown & Wexford, a company formed way back in 1854 as a subsidiary of the Irish South Eastern. The GS&WR absorbed the latter concern in 1863, declined to continue support of the Bagenalstown company, and the little company went bankrupt twelve months later. Surprisingly, it was resuscitated in 1866 by a London barrister, S. H. Motte. The reasons for this gentleman's action remain obscure, but he did purchase the derelict concern from GS&WR for £25,000, obtain a new Act, and proceed thereafter to form the Waterford, New Ross & Wexford (1866). Modest but important extensions were added; the company acquired new significance as the battle raged to reach Waterford, and in 1876 it was purchased jointly by GS&WR and DW&WR. Use of these metals, plus a further extension, brought the latter in 1887 to within 14 miles of Waterford. Then for diverse reasons further progress lengthened into yet another wearisome affair, and that last vital stage was not accomplished until February 1904. At first station facilities at Waterford had to be shared with GS&WR, then in 1906 the DW&WR opened its own. That same year GWR's long-standing ambition was also realised, when a $38\frac{1}{2}$-mile extention to Rosslare Harbour was opened to traffic. Fishguard and Cork were now in touch. Flushed with success, the DW&WR undertook one last change of name, and on 1 January 1907 became the Dublin & South Eastern Railway.

Established at last as one of Ireland's major

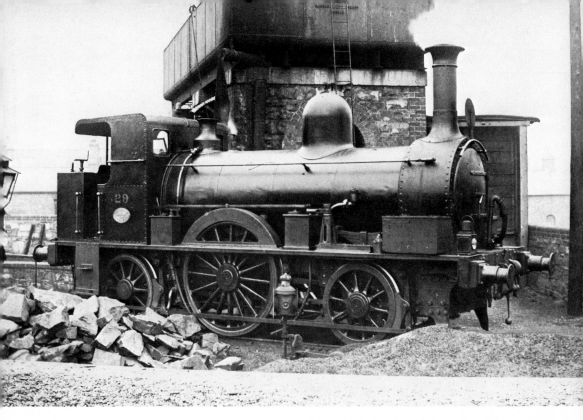

A delightful example of early Irish locomotive practice. DWWR 2–2–2T No 29, seen here at Dublin, was one of a fleet of well-tanks which handled suburban traffic between Dublin and Bray. Although some locomotives of this type lasted until 1924 none went into GSR stock. (*L&GRP*)

railways, the D&SER, one would have thought, had little to worry about. One hundred and fifty-six miles long, part of the Royal Mail route between Dublin and London, it even owned two termini in Ireland's capital, and its Grand Canal Street workshops, also at Dublin, could at least cope with half of its required locomotive construction. In reality, the opening decades of the 20th century brought many a sorrow. Arbitration proceedings had to be endured, disputes rose and fell thick as autumn leaves, and soil erosion along the Bray coast occasioned substantial and costly inland diversions. Then came the 'Troubles' of 1916. Tantamount with the declaration of an 'illegal' Republic. Wexford, Harcourt Street and Westland Row stations were seized by Irish Volunteers on 24 April. Indeed, the latter was held all through the rebellion. The munitions strike of 1920 helped little, and evening curfews imposed on Ireland's major cities had a deleterious effect on Dublin suburban traffic. Civil war followed in 1922, Wexford and Waterford being favoured targets. Damage done was later assessed at somewhere around £85,000, almost half the sum awarded to

the D&SER as government compensation after years of wartime control.

Post-war events have a habit of moving swiftly. Inevitable British railway amalgamations on 1 January 1923 clearly presaged similar developments in Ireland. The GS&WR and Cork & Bandon had already set the ball rolling by circularising their shareholders in May 1922 to similar effect. The D&SER declined to co-operate when approached, being more sympathetically inclined towards union with GNR(I). As a result the Great Southern Railway was formed on 12 November 1924 without it. A railway tribunal, left to persuade the D&SER of the error of its ways, now found it had a problem on its hands. Back in 1902 the LNWR (Euston) had contributed a loan of £100,000 towards completion of the New Ross–Waterford line. Over the years, too, a system had gradually evolved whereby cross-channel receipts were so apportioned that the D&SER received a virtual subsidy of £20,000 a year from the LNWR. Now, as a price of amalgamation the LNWR's successors, the LMSR, wanted repayment of its loan – or a seat on

Above: Ten DSER 0–6–0 tender locomotives entered GSR stock on 1 January 1925, and were sub-divided into five different classes. No 445 was one of a pair supplied by Beyer Peacock in 1905, whence it acquired the name *Cork*. For nearly 30 years these Class J8 locomotives were the only ones in Ireland with side-window cabs. This one was photographed at Broadstone in August 1957. (*J. L. Stevenson*)

Below: A view of Bray station, looking north, in September 1935. The Dublin & Wicklow Railway commenced operations between Dublin and Bray on 10 July 1854, but the platform on the right was not added by the GSR until 1927. (*T. Middlemass*)

Locomotives Built – 1853–64

Type	Fairbairn	Sharp Stewart	Vulcan Foundry	Neilson & Co	TOTALS	In Stock D&SER 1924	In Stock GSR 1925
2–2–2WT	4	—	4	8	16	—	—
2–4–0ST	—	—	2	—	2	—	—
2–4–0	4	3	—	—	7	3	1
0–4–2	—	9	—	—	9	2	—
Totals	8	12	6	8	34	5	1

the GSR Board. There was really little option left to the tribunal. On 1 January 1925 the D&SER joined the Irish combine which was restyled Great Southern Railways, and the LMSR was conceded its directorship.

Locomotives

Grouping in 1925 found the D&SER with 61 locomotives on hand. The fact that only 42 were taken into GSR stock is a clear indication of the D&SER's traditionally modest aspirations where motive power was concerned. For decades 0–4–2s and 2–4–0s had hauled their main line trains, while suburban duties between Harcourt Street and Bray were the prerogative of 2–2–2WT and 2–4–2T, and lighter and more frequent trains between Westland Row and Bray were entrusted to 2–2–2Ts and 2–4–0Ts. Even in 1924 tank locomotives of these four modest types constituted more than one-third of the D&SER's total stock. Some 4–4–0s had been added, and six-coupled locomotives had taken-over freight duties, but no single class in the D&SER's history ever exceeded 12 in number.

Grand Canal Street workshops were older than the D&SER itself. Purchased by the Dublin & Kingstown in 1837, nine locomotives were built there before the premises were leased in 1856 to

Locomotives Built – 1871–1924

Type	Grand Canal Street	Beyer Peacock	Sharp Stewart	Neilson & Co	Vulcan Foundry	Manning Wardle	TOTALS	In Stock D&SER 1924	In Stock GSR 1925
2–6–0	—	2	—	—	—	—	2	2	2
0–6–0	7	2	—	—	2	—	11	11	10
4–4–0	—	2	—	—	4	—	6	6	5
0–4–2	1	—	5	—	—	—	6	4	—
0–4–0T	—	—	—	—	—	2(a)	2	2	1
2–4–0T	8	3	—	—	—	—	11	11	4
2–4–2T	12	—	—	—	—	—	12	12	12
2–2–2WT	6	—	—	2	—	—	8	—	—
4–4–2T	1	2(b)	3	—	—	—	6	6	6
0–6–0T	—	—	—	—	—	1(c)	1	1	—
Totals	35	11	8	2	6	3	65	55	40

NOTES: (a) Steam railcars supplied in 1906. Not a success, and locomotive portions separated. One was sold to Dublin & Blessington Tramway for £800 in 1916; and later exchanged for a GS&WR locomotive.
(b) Last locomotive bought by the D&SER (1924).
(c) Contractor's locomotive absorbed in 1917.

Westland Row, the DSER's larger Dublin terminus, was extensively modernised in 1966. In this view, taken in March 1959, No 462, one of two 2–6–0s, designed by George Wild and built by Beyer Peacock in 1922, has arrived on a suburban working. These Class K2s were undoubtedly the DSER's finest locomotives, but post-war inflation took its toll when a quoted price of £13,350 per locomotive soared to £19,336 before delivery was effected. Westland Row, now known as Pearse, is no longer a terminus for main line services and is now only a through suburban station. (J. L. Stevenson)

the Dublin & Wicklow. By far the most distinctive was *Princess*, a 2–2–2T of 1841, the first locomotive in the world to be built by a railway company in its own workshops. As it was, the Dublin & Wicklow bought new from outside firms when it opened for business in 1854, and only in 1871 was locomotive construction resumed at Grand Canal Street. Conditions there were notoriously cramped and, as the following tables show, the D&SER was by no means able to

GSR Nos.	Type	Built by	Date	GSR Class	Class extinct
422	2–4–0	Sharp Stewart	1864	G7	1928
4 23–426	2–4–0T	Grand Canal St	1891–95	G1	1955
427	2–4–2T	Crewe	1896	F3	1936
428–433	2–4–2T	Grand Canal St	1886–96	F2	1957
434–439	2–4–2T	Grand Canal St	1901–08	F2	1953
440	0–6–0	Grand Canal St	1899	J20	1929
441	0–6–0	Grand Canal St	1900	J14	1935
442–444	0–6–0	Grand Canal St	1904–10	J8	1957
445–446	0–6–0	Beyer Peacock	1905	J8	1957
447	0–6–0	Vulcan Foundry	1891	J7	1930
448–449	0–6–0	Grand Canal St	1897	J1	1950
450–453	4–4–0	Vulcan Foundry	1895	D9	1940
454	4–4–0	Beyer Peacock	1905	D8	1949
445	4–4–2T	Grand Canal St	1911	C2	1959
456–457	4–4–2T	Beyer Peacock	1924	C2	1960
458–460	4–4–2T	Sharp Stewart	1893	C3	1960
461–462	2–6–0	Beyer Peacock	1922	K2	1965
Elf	0–4–0T	Manning Wardle	1906	M1	1931

dispense with outside assistance. Not surprisingly, Grand Canal Street shops were closed once the GSR took over in 1925.

In 1902 the D&SER also acquired six Webb 2–4–2Ts from the LNWR at a bargain price of £1,500 each, including re-gauging. During 1916/17 the government obliged the D&SER to return five to the UK for war work; back they went, again via Crewe for re-gauging! The sixth survived to become GSR No 427.

The GSR allocated running numbers 422 to 462, plus one name, to the 42 D&SER locomotives taken into stock. New classes created which consisted of only one locomotive did not last long in service.

During R. Cronin's long service as chief mechanical engineer (1897–1917) practically all D&SER locomotives bore names. Once G. H. Wild succeeded him, however, these were gradually removed, and by 1925 only five names remained. The GSR soon attended to their disposal.

Of the D&SER's two Dublin stations Westland Row, original terminal of the Dublin & Kingstown, gained precedence in later years, mainly because construction of the City of Dublin Junction Railway in 1891 linked it conveniently with the GNR(I), GS&WR and MGWR. Much less favourably sited, Harcourt Street, the Dublin & Wicklow's original terminus, possessed a second drawback in that the lines out of it climbed continuously for $4\frac{1}{2}$ miles. On 14 February 1900 a descending cattle train behind 0–6–0 No 17 failed to stop, and caused considerable alarm by ploughing through the buffers and station wall, to finish up suspended high over the public street. From then on a stop at Ranelagh, a half-mile out, was made compulsory for all trains.

Although the D&SER section continued to handle Dublin's most intensive suburban traffic, it became apparent by the 1930s that provision of two separate services between Dublin and Bray was uneconomic, in steam terms at least. Trials were held in 1932 with Drumm battery railcars, battery charging plants being installed at both Bray and Harcourt Street. The railcars proved very useful over the next decade and more, and were certainly a considerable improvement on Clayton steam coaches tried over the same ground in 1928. Nonetheless, the CIE withdrew the Drumm cars in July 1949. Diesel railcars and steam locomotives took their place, but the inevitable economics of road versus rail were already playing havoc with CIE resources, and on 1 January 1959 Harcourt Street station was closed. In summer 1960 further reductions were made in suburban services, and by then the last of D&SER's steam locomotives had gone.

CHAPTER TWO
GREAT SOUTHERN & WESTERN RAILWAY

Incorporated: 6 August 1844   *Opened:* 4 August 1846
Absorbed by Great Southern Railways: 30 June 1924

Undoubtedly Ireland's Premier Line, the GS&WR at its peak worked 1,150 route miles of track, one-third of the country's total; never once in its 80 years existence did it fail to pay a dividend. Yet much of Ireland's turbulent history is mirrored in its career, and the inevitable parabola which charted its fortunes held a greater than usual quotient of excitement and complication. Despite the GS&WR's inborn majesty, life was never simple.

When the Royal Commission of 1836 postulated a need for only two trunk lines to be constructed in Ireland, it presumed in its wisdom that canals and roads would take care of traffic to the west. Irish hearts felt differently, and were set from the outset on linking Dublin with the regional capitals of Cork, Waterford and Limerick. Consequently great public enthusiasm greeted the launching of a Great Leinster & Munster Railway in 1837. Totally ambitious though it was, the scheme failed to receive commensurate financial backing, and weakened additionally by uncertainty pending publication of the Commission's report, it fell by the wayside. Less than a decade later the dream was revived, and this time it bore the support of powerful elements in

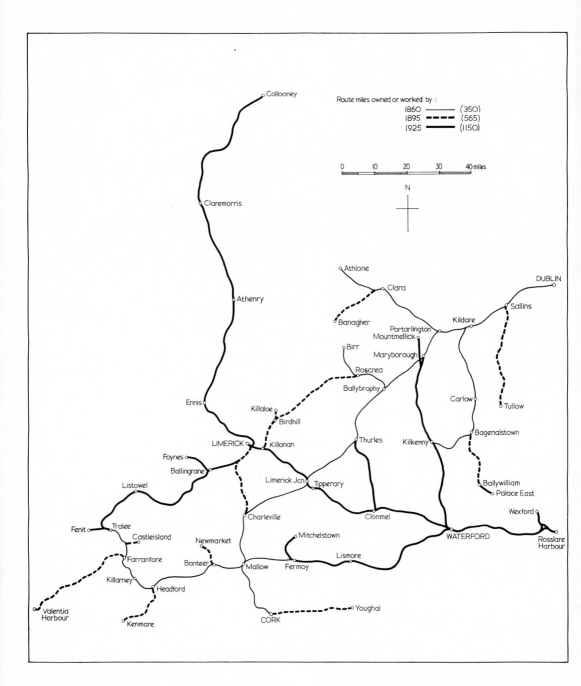

Route miles owned or worked by :
1860 ————— (350)
1895 ▬ ▬ ▬ (565)
1925 ▬▬▬▬ (1150)

0   10   20   30   40 miles

N

England's commercial world – the directors of the London & Birmingham Railway. Parliament readily gave its blessing, capital of £1,300,000 was quickly subscribed, and by January 1845 work was under way on a main line from Dublin to Cashel. A branch to Carlow, authorised by the same Bill, raised interesting evocations of earlier GL&MR ambitions.

The branch line was given priority, and on 4 August 1846 the GS&WR's first train ran from Dublin to Carlow. The 56-mile journey took $2\frac{1}{2}$ hours, but aided by connecting coach services even this laborious process immediately opened-up access to the South. By Act of 1845 Thurles was substituted for Cashel as the GS&WR's western goal, and despite difficulties, doubly

Left: Map showing the gradual expansion of the GS&WR during three main periods of development.

Above: Built in 1848 for the GSWR by Bury, Curtis & Kennedy of Liverpool, 2–2–2T No 36 was withdrawn in 1875 after completing almost half a million miles of main line service. Repaired many years later, and transferred to Cork (Glanmire Road) station in November on 1950, it is seen here displayed on a section of original GSWR heavy permanent way. Driving wheels are 6ft 0in in diameter, and overall weight is 22ton 19cwt. (*T. Middlemass*)

inflamed by the Great Famine, the 86½-mile main line from Dublin was completed by March 1848.

There was to be no respite. Hints from Cork that a local company might be formed to expedite rail communication between Cork and Limerick prompted the GS&WR management to entrust urgent construction of the remaining 78 miles from Thurles to one man, William Dargan. Taking on what was then a mammoth contract of £600,000, Dargan did not fail them. Limerick Junction was reached by July 1848, Mallow by 19 March 1849, and on 18 October 1849 a directors' special train steamed proudly from Dublin to Blackpool, a temporary terminus created in the outskirts of Cork. The through journey of 164 miles was accomplished in 5½ hours.

Meanwhile the GS&WR had taken pains to acquire half the capital of the Irish & South Eastern Railway. The latter had been created in 1845 as an amalgamation of the Great Leinster & Munster (1837), which owned an Act and nothing else, and the Wexford, Carlow & Dublin Junction

(1845), which had been led astray by earlier GWR (Paddington) enthusiasms. The ISER's sole constructional gambit consisted of linking Carlow with Lavistown Junction, via Bagenalstown, thereafter employing two miles running powers over the Waterford & Kilkenny metals to gain access to Kilkenny. For the time being the GS&WR was content to work the ISER line, and through service to Kilkenny was inaugurated on 12 November 1850. This brought route mileage under GS&WR control to a total of 209.

The story of how this mileage was increased to 350 by 1860 completes the first of three important epochs in the GS&WR's life. In 1856 powers obtained by the Mallow & Fermoy (1854) but never employed, were taken-over, and 17 miles of track were built. Thus an initial step in the GS&WR's ultimate drive towards Waterford was accomplished. A corresponding urge to forge north-west from its Cork–Dublin main line was not so easily satisfied, and as will be seen presently, upheaval brought about by the GS&WR's

Above: Limerick Junction, where the GSWR and WLWR met diagonally, was misleadingly named, for it was situated in Co Tipperary, and Limerick lay 22 miles away. Notorious for the complexity of its traffic arrangements, though these were eased in 1967, Limerick Junction required all stopping trains to reverse into its platforms. The famous crossing which permitted dual occupation of the main platform is just visible behind a Cork–Dublin train which has paused, in July 1938, before backing in. The locomotive is D17 4–4–0, No 9, an express design with 6ft 7in wheels, built by Aspinall immediately after MacDonnell's departure in 1883 but really a bogie version of the latter's last 2–4–0. (*T. Middlemass*)

Below: Limerick station itself was much more orthodox in layout and operation. This view was also taken in July 1938. The line to Newcastle and Tralee diverges to the right. (*T. Middlemass*)

ambition to reach Athlone and points north was the direct cause of the MGWR's formation in 1845. Yet, after much Parliamentary skirmishing, the GS&WR eventually acquired the right to link Portarlington with Athlone, and by October 1859 39 miles of new track were ready for traffic. Four years earlier the GS&WR had also absorbed the Roscrea & Parsonstown Junction Railway (1853). Having initially subscribed part of that concern's £100,000 capital, it saw in annexation of Roscrea metals a possible alternative approach to Limerick. The $22\frac{1}{2}$ miles from Ballybrophy to Parsonstown (later re-named Birr) were finally completed in March 1858.

Mallow to Killarney and Tralee, with rich prospects of tourist traffic, was the GS&WR's last bid before 1860 drew to a close. It was easily achieved by absorption of two companies whose original capitals held £100,000 GS&WR subscription. The Killarney Junction Railway (1846), with 41 miles from Mallow to Killarney — Dargan-built at a mere £5,000 per mile — opened in 1854, and had already established itself as a remarkably successful concern. Amongst other distinctions it owned Ireland's first railway-operated hotel. Its running partner, the Tralee & Killarney (1853), $21\frac{1}{2}$ miles long and also built by Dargan, fared less fortunately, and only provision of a £50,000 government loan ensured its completion in July 1859.

For the next 35 years the GS&WR, its basic railway framework firmly established, embarked on a policy of gentle but shrewd expansion. One or two new lines were constructed; others were acquired at bargain prices as smaller companies faltered. To start with, the Irish South Eastern was taken over on 1 July 1863, and tracks between Carlow and Lavistown Junction, previously worked by the GS&WR, now passed into direct possession. Progress further south from Bagenalstown came when, as already noted under D&SER affairs, the GS&WR approached the Public Works Loan Board in 1876, and purchased for £24,000 a half-interest in the moribund Waterford, New Ross & Wexford Junction Railway; $24\frac{1}{2}$ miles of strategic line to Ballywilliam were thus added to the GS&WR's growing network. Further techniques employed to advance the GS&WR route mileage to 565 during the 1860–95 phase can be summarised:

1864 Opened Roscrea–Birdhill extension
Part of the alternative drive to Limerick. This $32\frac{1}{4}$ mile extension linked up with Limerick & Castleconnell Railway at Birdhill, whence through service to Limerick became possible.

1866 Bought Cork & Youghal (1854)
27 miles, opened in stages between 1859 and 1861. The company's first chairman was Isaac Butt, Irish MP. Financially unsuccessful, the company was sold to the GS&WR for £310,000, *ie* half its construction cost. 10 locomotives, all Neilson-built, 25 carriages and 49 wagons were duly transferred. An important six miles between Cork and Cobh was also secured.

1871 Absorbed the Cork & Limerick Direct Railway (1860)
Nominally independent company, sponsored originally by the GS&WR. Its 25 miles between Charleville and Patrick's Well were worked from inception by the GS&WR. Running powers leased from the Limerick & Foynes gave access to Limerick.

1878 Declined to salvage the Parsonstown & Portumna Bridge Railway (1861)
12 miles, worked by the GS&WR from inception in 1868. When the company foundered the GS&WR stood aside, refusing to renew the lease. Appeals were made, unavailingly, to the government and in 1880 the railway was put up for auction by Public Works. In the absence of bidders it was abandoned in 1883, whence creditors promptly 'looted' it.

1879 Bought Castleisland Railway (1872)
First light railway in Ireland. The GS&WR declined to work the line when it opened in August 1875, but did build a special 'carriage engine' at Inchinore for use on its light metals. Once the GS&WR took command in 1879 two more such locomotives were supplied. Latterly traffic generated proved too much for them; heavier rails were laid, and conventional goods locomotives and tanks were employed.

1881 Absorbed Dublin & Baltinglass Junction Railway (1862/64)
Despite being the subject of two Bills, the company's proposed line between Naas and Baltinglass was never built — until the GS&WR obtained powers in 1881. Tracks were extended to Tullow in 1886. Total length was $34\frac{1}{4}$ miles.

1881 Absorbed Killorglin Railway (1871)
Formed to link Farranfore with Killorglin, but the $12\frac{1}{2}$-mile line was not constructed until authority was transferred to the GS&WR 10 years later.

First Irish railway to employ electric train staff system. When Allport Commission advocated extension to Valentia Harbour in 1888 the government backed the GS&WR's costs in building the requisite 27 miles with a £85,000 grant. Valentia, most westernly railhead in Europe, was opened to traffic on 12 September 1893.

1893 Opened Headford–Kenmare extension
In 1880s the Cork & Macroom and GS&WR competed in proposing lines to Kenmare. With the Macroom railway unable to implement its ambition, the GS&WR obtained requisite authority in 1884. Again, construction costs of this wild barren 19¾-mile section were borne by the government, this time to the tune of £50,000.

1892 Bought Kanturk & Newmarket (1887)
8¾-mile line between Banteer and Newmarket, worked by the GS&WR from its opening in 1889. Maintenance sadly neglected, and GS&WR, after threatening to cease the working, purchased the threadbare concern for £58,000.

1895 Bought Clara & Banagher (1890) formerly Midland Counties & Shannon Junction (1861)
19 miles, worked by the GS&WR 10 years from opening in 1884. Bought for £5,000 from Board of Works, to whom the C&BR owed £68,000.

By the end of 1895 the GS&WR owned 565½

route miles, worked another 40¼ miles, but yearned still to establish positive links between Dublin, Wexford, Waterford, Cork, Limerick, Tralee and Sligo. Few people could have guessed that the passage of a few more years would see that ambition achieved. The explosion started in 1898, gained momentum during 1900–02, and long before final accounts were published in June 1924, the GS&WR had succeeded in doubling its mileage.

A solution to the Waterford – Kilkenny – Dublin problem was obtained on 1 July 1900, when the GS&WR absorbed the Waterford & Kilkenny Railway. Unusually, this Irish railway, incorporated in 1845, was owned by Bristol shareholders in the main, and maintained its registered office in London. Apart from suffering the disadvantage of having to operate by remote control, the W&KR's original London board further distinguished itself by proposing to lay Prosser's Patent wooden rails, with guide wheels on locomotives and coaches. The Board of Trade, while not objecting *per se* to this remarkable proposition, pointed out that adoption of such a practice would inhibit future through working. The company, taking the hint, obtained a fresh Act in 1850, and paid £15,000 to be released from the Prosser contract. Its subsequent fortunes were no more inspired. Initial progress in building the 30-mile line was slow, and even after completion

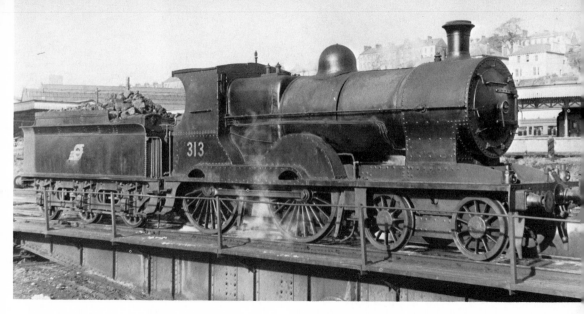

Left: Two years after launching his D17s Aspinall, introduced a larger version, the D14, and Nos 88 and 89, were subsequently rebuilt with new frames, cut-away splashers and new cab. No 89 was reclassified D13 between 1925 and 1933, but had reverted to Class D14 by the time it was photographed at Dun Laoghaire in October 1956. (*J. L. Stevenson*)

Above: Class D10, No 313, seen at Glanmire Road, Cork in 1956, was a Coey product of 1903, and suffered the ignomiry of being sold to Spain for scrap in 1958. (*J. L. Stevenson*)

endless inter-company squabbles waxed at both the Kilkenney and Waterford ends. The Waterford & Limerick Railway, which had undertaken in 1860 to work the line, refused to renew the lease when it expired five years later, and the W&KR was left to soldier on as best it could.

Meanwhile the Kilkenny Junction Railway (1860) had succeeded, after several false starts, in linking Kilkenny to Portlaoise, a short distance from the GS&WR's main line at Maryborough. Worked from its inception by the W&KR, traffic commenced in May 1867, by which time the W&KR and KJR had acquired ambitious joint powers to construct a Central Ireland line from Maryborough to Geashill, on the GS&WR Athlone branch. In anticipation of the event, and encouraged by Paddington aspirations to see cattle traffic drawn to Waterford, the W&KR changed its name in 1868 to Waterford & Central Ireland. A truncated $7\frac{1}{2}$-mile section to Mountmellick was opened in March 1885, thanks mainly to a subscription of £40,000 from Paddington. But there the dream ended. The CIR was absorbed by the W&CIR in 1877, the KJR following in 1896. On 1 July 1900 the GS&WR in turn absorbed the W&CIR. The GWR investment in setting-up the CIR was revalued at £27,480, and for the next 25 years payment of this sum to Paddington was shown as a separate item in GS&WR annual accounts.

During its lifetime the W&CIR employed 16 locomotives. Its initial trio of 4–2–2Ts, built by C. Tayleur & Co in 1848, were the first side tanks in the world, albeit they were much too modestly powered, even for Irish purposes. Nine locomotives were handed over to the GS&WR in 1900, and all had perished by 1910. The ultimate survivor, No 4, Vulcan-built in 1897, was the last 0–4–2 built for any British railway.

A massive addition of mileage came GS&WR's way on 1 January 1901, when it absorbed the Waterford & Limerick Railway, which was then the fourth largest railway in Ireland. Though the principal offices of this company were situated in Waterford, its 'heart' lay in Limerick, as did its locomotive and carriage works. The initial section between Limerick and Tipperary was opened after considerable difficulty in May 1848. Ultimately, mainly by dint of a government loan, Limerick and Waterford, $77\frac{1}{4}$ miles apart, were linked in September 1854. The W&LR, leading a frugal existence, leaned heavily on loans and traffic rebates which sprang from close initial associations with the GWR in England. Later, when GWR policy changed, the W&LR was obliged to seek a new partner; hence its ultimate fusion with the GS&WR. Ironically, a previous attempt in 1860 to amalgamate with the GS&WR had failed. An interesting W&LR hallmark was the penchant it constantly exhibited, despite its

Above: Trouble at Limerick Junction in pre-GSR days as No 56 is re-railed after coming off on a set of points. (*L&GRP*)

Top left: Best loved of all Irish locomotives were the GSWR's 101 Class 0–6–0s, later classified J15 by the GSR. Introduced by MacDonnell in 1866, 111 were built between then and 1903. Even 80 years after their introduction 96 were still serving, although 61 had modern superheated boilers. They could be found everywhere on the southern Irish system. Reboilered, and with Belpaire firebox, No 171 arrives at Cahir with a Limerick Junction train on 4 July 1938. (*T. Middlemass*)

Left: No 182, in original form with oven-type smokebox doors, takes water at Farranfore in March 1935 before backing on to its train. (*T. Middlemass*)

own poverty, for working other companies' lines. In 1900, for instance, only half the $342\frac{1}{2}$ miles it operated actually lay in its possession. The situation is best understood by considering separately the W&LR's twin drives from Limerick to Tralee, and Sligo.

The W&LR was closely involved in the creation of the Limerick & Castleconnel Railway (1856), and a proposal in 1858 to extend to Killaloe attracted investment of £10,000 from the MGWR, which was at that time at cross purposes with the GS&WR. Once relations improved in 1860 the MGWR transferred its L&CR holding to the GS&WR which then, by means of the Birdhill extension, secured entry into Limerick. Fourteen miles long, and built cheaply at £5,000 per mile, the L&CR was worked from its inception by the W&LR, and was taken-over by it in 1872.

W&LR's drive SW to Tralee opened in 1873, and continued in stages:

1872 Absorbed Limerick & Foynes (1853)
Opened in 1856. One-third of the capital was held by William Dargan, and the remainder by the GS&WR and W&LR. 26 miles long, operated from inception by W&LR.

1867 Worked Rathkeale & Newcastle Junction (1861)

Above: H. A. Ivatt's main contribution to locomotive policy during his decade of service with the GSWR lay in introducing new tank types. No 35, a Class F6 2—4—2T, was one of six built at Inchicore in 1892—94. With 20 years of service still ahead, it is seen shunting at Limerick in July 1938. (*T. Middlemass*)

Below: A tank oddity on the GSWR; 0—4—2 saddle tank *Sambo*, built in 1914, spent all its life shunting at Inchicore and is seen there in August 1956. (*J. L. Stevenson*)

10½ miles, from Ballingrane (L&FR) to Newcastle West. Though worked by the W&LR, it retained independence until taken-over by the GS&WR in January 1902.

1880 Worked Limerick & Kerry (1873)
Completed link between Newcastle West and the GS&WR at Tralee, in 1880. 43 miles, worked by the W&LR, but independence retained until absorption by the GS&WR in January 1902 was effected by payment of £40,000 to liquidators.

1887 Worked Tralee & Fenit (1880)
Eight miles long, opened 1887. Worked by the W&LR, but absorbed by the GS&WR in 1901.

A W&LR route from Limerick to Sligo was achieved mainly by absorptions:

1874 Absorbed Limerick & Ennis (1846)
Formerly Limerick, Ennis & Killaloe, but the name was changed when lapsed powers were revived in 1853. 24¾ miles, opened 1859, and worked by the W&LR, except for one year.

1893 Absorbed Athenry & Ennis Junction (1859)
36 miles long. Opened 1869, and leased in 1872 to the W&LR.

1893 Absorbed Athenry & Tuam (1858)
Another 15½ miles toward Sligo. Opened 1860, leased for 10 years to the MGWR, thereafter to the W&LR.

Through services between Limerick and Sligo became feasible when the Athenry & Tuam Extension to Claremorris Light Railway built 17 miles to Claremorris in 1894, and was further developed to join with the MGWR at Coolooney. The latter 47 miles, built with the aid of state funds, were worked by the W&LR from completion in October 1895, and running powers over six miles of MGWR metals gave the W&LR direct access to Sligo. Three months later the W&LR, conscious of its new found prestige, changed its name, and from 1 January 1896 became known as the Waterford, Limerick & Western Railway. The A&TECLR retained its independence until it was absorbed by the GSR on 1 January 1925.

One more railway worked by the W&LR remains to be considered. This was the ambitious Southern Railway, authorised by Act of 1865 to link Thurles with Clonmel and Youghal. So precarious were company finances that only the 25½ miles separating Thurles and Clonmel were

ever built, and that took 15 years to achieve. The W&LR worked the line until operations were transferred to the GS&WR in 1901, by which time the SR, through default, had passed into possession of the Board of Works. Inability in the long run to identify shareholders in the unfortunate concern delayed vesting of the SR into the GSR until 17 November 1925.

When the WL&WR was absorbed by GS&WR on 1 January 1901 58 locomotives, mostly Dübs, Kitson, and Vulcan products, 159 coaches and 1,350 wagons were duly handed-over. M. Atock acted as locomotive superintendent from 1861 to 1872, before leaving for like duties with the MGWR; but J. G. Robinson, appointed in 1889, played the key role in modernising the W&LR stock. Chimneys with copper caps were an interesting evocation of Robinson's earlier days at Swindon. The quality of his work was not lost on Manchester, where from 1900 onwards he pursued an illustrious career with the GCR at Gorton. All ex-W&LR locomotives, 20 in number, which passed into GSR stock in 1925 were built during the Robinson régime. Even by 1948 12 still survived.

During this epoch the GS&WR also turned its attention towards extending east from Fermoy, towards Waterford and Wexford. Various acquisitions ensued:

1898 Absorbed Waterford, Dungarvan & Lismore (1872) also Fermoy & Lismore (1869)
Purchases made to further collusion between the GS&WR and GWR in reaching Waterford. Both minor lines were already worked by WD&LR, which had fallen on hard times. Their joint 59¼ miles closed the gap between Fermoy and Waterford. Seven locomotives acquired by the GS&WR from the WD&LR were soon withdrawn.

1898 Absorbed Waterford & Wexford (1864)
Not opened until 1882; then only parts completed were a pier at Rosslare and six miles therefrom to DW&WR metals at Wexford. Train service ceased in May 1889, and was not resumed until the Fishguard & Rosslare Co took over in August 1894. Four years later the working was handed over to the GS&WR.

1900 Absorbed Mitchelstown & Fermoy (1891)
12 miles long. Opened 1891, worked and maintained by the GS&WR. Vested in the GS&WR from 1900, until closed in 1963.

Right: Classified E3 by the GSR, MacDonnell's classic 0–4–4 well-tanks specialised in cross-country service. No 51 is seen at Ennis in September 1931. (*L&GRP*)

Below right: The influence of Paddington on Waterford & Limerick Railway affairs is easily detected in this study of No 11, a WLWR 2–4–0 of 1890 vintage. (*L&GRP*)

Below: Another GSWR oddity. In October 1956 0–6–0 saddle tank No 299 was photographed at Albert Quay, Cork. A product of 1892, originally named *Shamrock*, this locomotive came to the GSWR via the Fenit Harbour Commission. Behind stands No 269, one of four ex-WLWR 4–4–2 tanks which survived to be taken over by CIE. By the end of 1957 all had gone. (*J. L. Stevenson*)

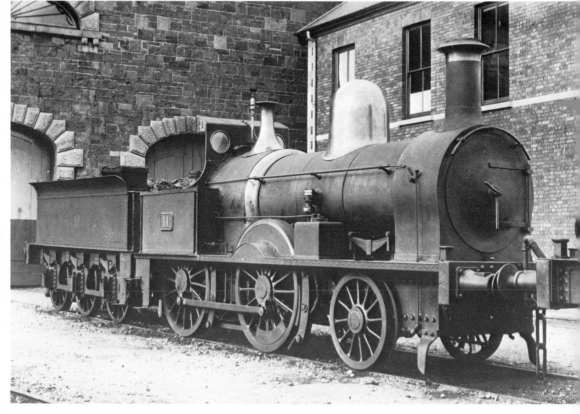

1902 Acquired Ballywilliam & Palace East section
A $3\frac{1}{4}$-mile section, part of the DW&WR's
purchase from Public Works in 1876, when part of
the WNR&WJR also fell into GS&WR hands.
This short stretch proved awkward for the
DW&WR to handle, and was transferred to the
GS&WR in 1902.

On the domestic front the GS&WR made two
modest moves. In 1900 it absorbed the
Drumcondra & North Dublin Link (1894). This
suburban route had been planned to connect
Glasnevin with the GS&WR freight yards at
Dublin's North Wall. The promoters were unable
to raise capital, and the two-mile link was
completed by the GS&WR in April 1901.

Word War I saw final developments, when coal
shortages in Ireland obliged the government to
finance construction of railway lines into two
Kilkenny coalfields. A 10-mile line from Athy to
Wolfhill was opened in September 1918, by dint of
'borrowing' sleepers and rails from the GS&WR
Athy-Carlow section, which now became single-
tracked. Its active life was short, and it was later
reduced to a mere stump of one mile. The other
colliery line, also worked by the GS&WR, ran
from a junction north of Kilkenny to Castlecomer
and Deerpark Colliery. The last standard gauge
line to be opened in Ireland, and heavily graded in
parts, it was opened in September 1919. Up to
1931 light passenger traffic was also
accommodated; sporadic coal traffic lingered until
1 January 1963, when the 17-mile line was closed.
Both colliery lines were vested in the GSR on 1
January 1929.

Locomotives

The history of locomotive construction on the
GS&WR is quite clear-cut. During the railway's
initial decade all locomotives were supplied by
private builders, 59 in total. Once the company's
own works at Inchicore got into its stride in 1852
an increasing flow of home-built products
emerged, and of 400 GS&WR locomotives built
between 1852 and 1924 over 90 per cent owed
their origin to Inchicore. All locomotives shown in
Table 1 below were withdrawn between 1869 and
1879.

For a variety of reasons, locomotive practice on
a number of Irish railways was influenced by that
of English contemporaries. Locomotive styles on
the WL&WR, GNR(I), and NCC, for example,
borrowed much from the GWR, GNR and MR
respectively. So, too, motive power on the
GS&WR emulated that of Crewe, and latterly of
Beyer Peacock, to a marked degree. It is only when
the line of successive GS&WR locomotive
superintendents is examined that the true resilience
of the affinity emerges. The 'inbreeding' it reveals
is remarkable.

First to serve as GS&WR locomotive engineer,
John Dewrance, ex-Liverpool & Manchester
Railway, may or may not have had some say in the
matter when the GS&WR directors ordered
locomotives direct from Bury, Curtis & Kennedy
in 1845. What is worth noting is that J. E.
McConnell, Cork-born and famous latterly for his
LNWR 'Bloomers', not only served as foreman a
decade earlier at Bury's Liverpool works, but went
on to succeed Edward Bury in 1847 as locomotive
superintendent at Wolverton. Thus soon does the

(1) GS&WR Locomotives – Private Builders – 1845–1856

Built by	Passenger locomotives		Date	Goods locomotives	Totals
	2–2–2	2–4–0		0–4–2	
Bury, Curtis & Kennedy	20	10	1845–48	—	30
Sharp, Stewart	20	—	1846–48	—	20
Grendon	—	—	1849	2	2
Rothwells	—	—	1849	4	4
Fairbairn	—	2	1855–56	1	3
Totals	40	12		7	59

Above: Seven large 0–6–0s introduced by Coey in 1903 proved too heavy at the front end and, re-entering Inchicore, they emerged a second time as Ireland's first standard-gauge Moguls. Later superheated, they proved extremely popular on heavy main line goods work. Class K3 No 361 is seen at Tralee in August 1957. (*J. L. Stevenson*)

Below: No 405 approaches Limerick Junction with a Dublin–Cork express in July 1938. Constructed at Inchicore Works in 1921 with four cylinders, it was later rebuilt in two-cylinder form. After Mallow viaduct was destroyed by Republican forces in August 1922, No 405 hauled President Cosgrave's inaugural train over the new viaduct in October 1923. (*T. Middlemass*)

(2) GS&WR Locomotives Built at Inchicore – 1852–1924

	Passenger locomotives						Goods locomotives				
	2–2–2	2–4–0	4–4–0	4–6–0	Totals		0–4–2	0–6–0	4–6–0	2–6–0	Totals
	13	35	76	4	128		19	129	7	4	159
Dates built	1853 –63	1868 –75	1877 –1913	1916 –23			1852 –65	1854 –1914	1905 –24	1909	

	Tank locomotives										
	0–2–4	0–4–4	0–4–2ST	0–6–4	2–4–2	4–4–2	0–4–2	0–6–2	4–8–0	0–6–0	Totals
	1	35	5	6	6	10	1	—	2	12	78
Dates built	1857	1869 –87	1875 –1914	1876 –80	1892 –94	1894 –1900	1894	— —	1915 –24	1887 –90	

LNWR syndrome crop up in GS&WR history.

When Dewrance defected to the MGWR in 1847, the man appointed to succeed him was G. M. Miller, the GS&WR civil engineer, who had previously worked with Robert Stephenson on the London & Birmingham Railway. Miller ordered a few locomotives from private sources; more importantly, it was during his reign that production at the GS&WR's new workshops at Inchicore commenced in 1852. While it is generally conceded that John Wakefield, his assistant, was largely responsible for locomotive design, the fact remains that by the time Miller died at an early age in 1864 main line trains on the GS&WR were being exclusively worked by a dozen single-wheelers, all built at Inchicore, and bearing a close resemblance to McConnell's 'Bloomers'. Eight 0–6–0s were also produced, but no tank engines appeared on GS&WR metals until 1866, when a handful of saddletanks were acquired through absorption of the Cork & Youghal Railway.

After Miller came Alexander Macdonnell. Not only a meticulous and efficient engineer, Macdonnell was already deeply influenced by Ramsbottom locomotive design. By this time the GS&WR track had acquired an evil reputation, and broken locomotive springs were an ever-present hazard. Given appropriate latitude by his new employers, Macdonnell spared no effort in pulling GS&WR locomotive policy together. His first locomotives in 1866 were 0–6–0s, and so successful was the class (101, later J15) that 111 of them were built over the years to 1903. They were modelled closely on the DX class which Ramsbottom constructed by the hundred at Crewe; the main difference was the oven-type smokebox doors favoured by Macdonnell. Interestingly, cast metal numberplates, generally accepted to be of LNWR derivation, were introduced by Macdonnell on GS&WR locomotives some years before Webb arrived at Crewe. Macdonnell's first express locomotives, 2–4–0s produced in 1869, were again very

(3) GS&WR Locomotives – Private Builders – 1867–1923

Built by	Passenger locomotives		Goods locomotives	Tank locomotives	Totals	Dates built
	4–4–0	4–6–0	0–6–0	0–6–2	—	—
Neilson & Co	6	—	—	—	6	1902
Armstrong	—	6	—	—	6	1916–23
Beyer Peacock	—	—	12	—	12	1867–73
NB Loco Co	—	—	7	4	11	1903
Totals	6	6	19	4	35	—

Top: Former Great Southern & Western six-wheeled first class coach of the last century downgraded to third class and still in use in the Cork area on excursion work in the 1950s.

Above: Two Great Southern & Western corridor thirds built around the first decade of the present century and seen here at Cobh on a local train from Cork in the mid-1950s. Notice the water tanks for the toilets protruding above roof level; the far coach retains gas lighting.

Below: A Great Southern & Western non-gangwayed lavatory brake composite with clerestory roof. Although dating from the turn of the century this vehicle includes a number of internal features predating practice of later years, including an end entrance vestibule with side corridor to the first class compartment and toilet at the far end, and centre corridor third class accommodation in the middle leading to a toilet compartment next to the guard's van. (G. M. Kichenside)

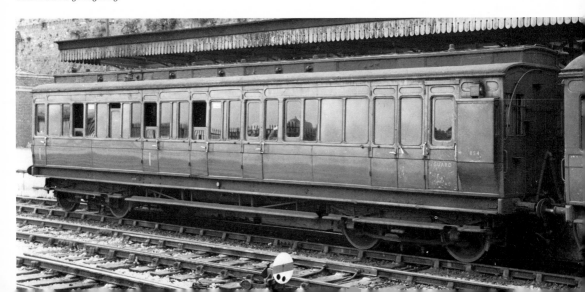

Ramsbottom-like in appearance, as was a smaller version which followed for local work. 1869 also saw the introduction of 0–4–4Ts, and production of this useful type was continued by his successors up to 1899. In 1876 Macdonnell produced the first standard-gauge 0–6–4Ts in the British Isles, though later they were rebuilt as 0–6–0Ts. Another type of 0–6–4T appeared in 1880, but these were really rail-motors for use on the Castleisland line. A year previously he had abandoned the 2–4–0 design, and had introduced in lieu his famous 'Kerry Bogie' 4–4–0s. Mostly employed around Cork, these delightful little locomotives incorporated first use in the UK of the swing-link bogie. Later its employment spread to England, through Macdonnell (NER 1884), Aspinall (L&YR 1887) and Ivatt (GNR 1896). Certainly by the time Macdonnell left GS&WR employment to advance his career with the NER locomotive affairs at Inchicore had improved beyond recognition. Ironically, the very sweep of Macdonnell's methods antagonised Gateshead men, and his stay there was both short and unhappy.

Still LNWR influence persisted at Inchicore: for Macdonnell's successor was his assistant, J. A. F. Aspinall, and the latter's training had been obtained under both Ramsbottom and Webb. A large 4–4–0 for express work and more 0–4–4Ts were produced at Inchicore before Aspinall left in July 1886 to take up duties with L&YR at Horwich. Aspinall's manager and close friend, H. A. Ivatt, took his job; significantly, he too, had served an apprenticeship under Webb. No express or goods tender locomotives were designed during his term as locomotive superintendent, but he did introduce new tank types, for example 2–4–2Ts in 1892 and 4–4–2Ts in 1894. He also experimented with compounding; the two locomotives concerned, a 4–4–0 and 0–6–0, were later restored to their original form. In 1895 Ivatt moved to Doncaster in succession to Patrick Stirling.

The appointment at Inchicore was given to his assistant, R. Coey, who had been with the GS&WR since 1876. By now GS&WR trains were increasing rapidly in weight, and Coey struck a new line in developing new powerful 4–4–0s. Thirty-four, of varying categories, were built between 1900 and 1908. Dished smokeboxes were introduced, a 26in stroke was employed, one locomotive was given a taper boiler, and four were even given names. On the goods traffic side Coey produced a last twelve class 101 0–6–0s, and introduced four more of a slightly larger variety in 1903. Seven even larger 0–6–0s, built the same year, later became first Moguls in Ireland when they were rebuilt at Inchicore to relieve excess leading weight. Coey also introduced Ireland's first 4–6–0 tender locomotives in 1905, and four years later followed-up with four very satisfactory 2–6–0s. His tank engines were few in number: a quartet of Atlantic tanks in 1900, followed by four more in 1902. These latter were the last passenger tanks built by the GS&WR. Four 0–6–2Ts were out-shopped in 1903, but led undistinguished careers.

Coey's successor in 1911, R. E. L. Maunsell, a pupil of Ivatt, only remained with the GS&WR for two years before moving on to the SECR in 1913. During his brief spell Maunsell introduced the Schmidt superheater, built a dozen excellent 0–6–0s, and attracted great attention by building a 'super' 4–4–0 at Inchicore – No 341 *Sir William Goulding*.

Although the man who succeeded Maunsell had only served two years with the GS&WR, he brought to Inchicore wide and refreshing experience of railway practice elsewhere: E. A. Watson had already worked in the USA and at Swindon. His major contribution during eight years at Inchicore was to reduce the incidence of double-heading, by building Ireland's first six-coupled passenger locomotives. No 400 emerged in 1916, with a boiler pressure of 175lb/sq in, and nine more followed. His only other design, a 4–8–0T for banking duties, did not meet with the same success. In 1921 Watson left to become general manager of Beyer Peacock & Co, but died shortly afterwards.

The last holder of the GS&WR's new title of chief mechanical engineer was J. R. Bazin, who had also trained under Ivatt at Doncaster, and understood the beauty of simplicity in design. His sole new design for the GS&WR was a class of three 2-cylinder 4–6–0s, brought out in 1924 for fast goods service, but soon promoted to passenger traffic. Then when the GS&WR lost its independence in June 1924 Bazin was appointed first CME of the Great Southern Railway.

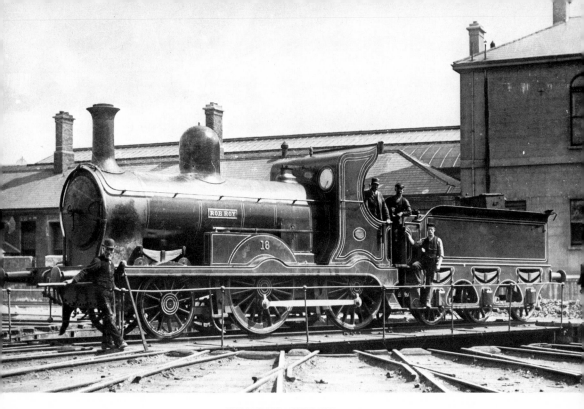

CHAPTER THREE
MIDLAND GREAT WESTERN RAILWAY

Incorporated: 21 July 1845   *Opened:* 28 June 1847
Absorbed by the Great Southern Railway: 12 November 1924

Born out of controversy, the MGWR went on to become in many ways the most Irish railway of all. Its locomotive practice, for instance, owed nothing to external persuasions, and in their heyday MGWR locomotives, liveried in emerald green, were quite unmistakable. Long bell-mouthed chimneys vied in handsomeness with curved cabs whose roofs flared upwards at the rear, while locomotive names, lavished with a generosity unparalleled elsewhere in the United Kingdom, shone from plates mounted on the boiler sides, below the dome. MGWR locomotives had no need for lamp brackets in front of the chimney, for headcodes on that railway required only one lamp, or two. Indeed even in recent years headcodes in Ireland, certainly in the Republic, owed little to the British classification.

It might also be said of the MGWR that it tried hard to confine its activities to an area defined by its title. Yet even this was no easy task, for in the formative years much valuable energy was expended battling with its arch-enemy, the

GS&WR. The process started in 1845, when disputes over a proposed new line from Dublin to Mullingar and points west provoked an angry split on the GS&WR Board. The dissentients broke away, and after considerable Parliamentary maneouvering they succeeded in obtaining an Act to construct the MGWR – *and* purchase the Royal Canal. The latter, $96\frac{1}{4}$ miles long, and said to have cost £$1\frac{1}{2}$ million, dated back to 1789. The MGWR, bent on following its easy course when constructing the Dublin–Mullingar line, bought it for £298,059, though new ownership carried only the right to levy tolls, not to act as carriers. Later the MGWR provoked the GS&WR further by attempting to buy the Grand Canal, which linked

Above: The classic flare of the cab roof shows to full advantage in this view of MGWR 2–4–0 No 18 *Rob Roy* as does the pride of the engine crew. Note the absence of a lamp bracket in front of the chimney. On the railways now part of CIE, except the Great Northern, steam locomotives normally had lamp positions only over the buffers, as the headcode did not conform to the British code. Green lights supplemented white for variations. (*L&GRP*)

Above: Built by the MGWR in the 1890s, No 654, formerly No 28 *Clara*, and by then GSR Class G2, had altered somewhat in appearance by 1962. The oldest passenger class when grouping was effected in 1925, all but one G2 served the GSR faithfully into the 1950s. No 583, the J18 seen approaching, carried the name *Clonbrook* in earlier days. Twenty-three of the class emerged from Broadstone in 1876–95; tough, versatile locomotives, the last was not withdrawn until 1965. (*J. L. Stevenson*)

Below: When the GSR was formed on 1 January 1925 the MGWR handed-over 82 0–6–0s of various types. Its most modern class was J5, 23 of which were built between 1921 and 1924. Significantly, they were never named. No 627 is seen here at Mullingar in August 1958. (*J. L. Stevenson*)

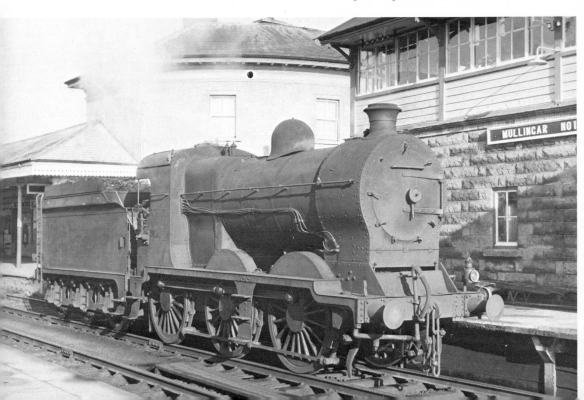

Dublin with the River Shannon. Sustained pressure by the larger company succeeded in limiting MGWR interests to a seven-year lease. More petty and expensive squabbling ensued, until arbitration in 1860 restored order between the two companies.

Meanwhile, all was not light and sweet reason in the MGWR boardroom; ambitions to extend further west to Athlone and Galway generated such friction in turn among the MGWR directors that some defected to sponsor an Irish Great Western Railway. A delighted GS&WR offered every assistance to the rebels, some dubious canvassing went on at Westminster, and only by deleting Athlone temporarily from the plans was the MGWR able to outwit the IGWR splinter group. The following year, 1846, the MGWR won a second battle, by gaining access to Athlone. The IGWR counter-Bill was rejected in the Commons, much to the chagrin of the GS&WR directors, who promptly resorted to supporting the Grand Junction Railway, a new concern designed expressly to bite deeply into MGWR territory. Rebuff from Westminster came GS&WR's way yet again.

Thereafter, despite financial stringencies induced by the Great Famine, the MGWR pressed on, and aided by a government loan of £500,000 succeeded in reaching Galway by 1851. Six years later the GS&WR, unabashed, returned to the fray by backing another new venture, the Great Northern & Western Railway. The avowed aim of the latter was to link Athlone with Roscommon and Castlerea. This fresh exacerbation saw relations between the two major companies flare into outright war. Fortunately, resort to arbitration in 1860 introduced wiser and cooler counsels and as a result of its findings the GS&WR and MGWR agreed to respect an arrangement whereby traffic into Athlone would be shared. The GN&WR was leased in 1870 to the MGWR, which twenty years later graduated to full ownership of the Athlone–Westport route. An MGWR branch from Manula and Killala was somewhat laboriously completed in 1893, and within two years 27 miles of track were laid across the wild country which separated Westport and Achill.

Curiously enough, despite the impetuous nature of MGWR origins in 1845, wholly ten years elapsed before the sanctioned branch line from Mullingar to Longford was completed. From there the natural target was construction of a main line to Sligo. Appropriate powers were obtained in 1857, and the 57-mile extension was opened to traffic in September 1862. The 51 miles to Collooney were single track only, but at least Sligo got its railway. Meanwhile, a branch line from Inny Junction to Cavan, 25 miles distant, had been completed in 1856. Seven years later GNR(I) linked Cavan with Clones, and later MGWR added a modest branch between Crossdoney and Killeshandra.

The armistice of 1860 proved doubly valuable for it enabled both the MGWR and GS&WR to embark on policies of gentle expansion. The MGWR was the more modest of the two. The route between Dublin and Galway continued to form the backbone of the MGWR system, and branches in the main ran north therefrom. 'Crack' trains were allowed five hours to traverse the MGWR 126½-mile main line. Subsequent peaceful developments led to the MGWR ultimate route mileage of 538:

1873 Opened Streamstown & Clara branch
Seven miles. Connected with the GS&WR at Clara, where the MGWR had its own station.

1877 Absorbed Sligo & Ballaghaderreen Railway (1863)
Nine miles, leading from Kilfree Junction. Opened 1874, and worked by the MGWR until vested in it 1877.

1877 Opened Enfield & Edenderry branch
A branch, 10 miles long, west of Dublin. Passenger services ceased in 1931, and the branch was closed in 1963.

1888 Absorbed Dublin & Meath (1858)
North to Navan. 35 miles long, worked by the MGWR from 1869. Also owned a 12-mile branch from Kilmessan to Attboy, opened in 1864.

1888 Absorbed Navan & Kingscourt (1865)
11-mile extension of the D&MR, worked by the MGWR from 1875. No rail link was ever established between Kingscourt and GNR(I) at neighbouring Carrickmacross.

1890 Sponsored Loughrea & Attymon Light Railway (1889)
12-mile branch off Galway line at Attymon. Built under Light Railways & Tramways Act of 1883. Opened 1890.

1892 Worked Ballinrobe & Claremorris Light Railway (1884)
13-mile light railway off the Westport line, opened

Above: Athlone, 1958: a weatherbeaten white disc on the tender reminds us that No 582, Class J18, was one of 90 locomotives converted to oil-burning during 1945–48 when coal supply was difficult in the Irish Free State. A similar disc on the smokebox front warned signalmen to concede preference to these locomotives. (*J. L. Stevenson*)

Below: 'Achill Bogie' 4–4–0 No 532, of Class D16 introduced by the MGWR in 1900, was active enough when seen at Westport in July 1938, but by 1956 was reduced to raising steam at Broadstone and was condemned twelve months later. (*J. L. Stevenson*)

Above: With no suburban traffic demands to meet around Dublin the MGWR saw little value in building passenger tank locomotives, and latterly only two series of 0–6–0 tanks were constructed. One of 12 introduced in 1891, No 554, ex-*Fly* shunts a coach at Galway in August 1957. (*J. L. Stevenson*)

Below: Nominally a rebuild from a 2–4–0 named *St Patrick*, No 541, duly equipped with 6ft 3in driving wheels for express work, was one of nine 4–4–0s turned out from Broadstone between 1910 and 1915, and is seen here at North Wall in August 1957. By 1959 the whole class (GSR D6) had gone. (*J. L. Stevenson*)

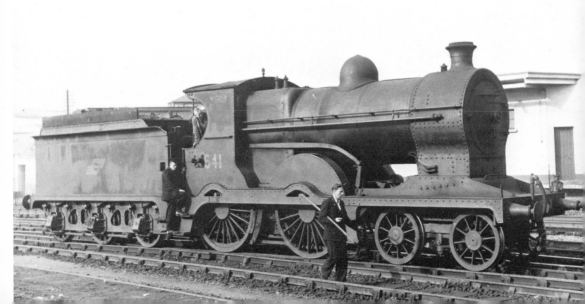

1892. The company retained its independence until absorbed by the GSR in 1925.

1895 Opened Galway–Clifden Extension
49 miles long. Built rapidly to attract tourist traffic to Connemara.

Thus, the MGWR formed an extremely serviceable and compact unit long before events in 1924 obliged it to join the larger national complex known as the Great Southern Railway. Yet within a decade of the GSR's formation financial hardships of the 1930s began to undermine Irish railways, as elsewhere. Axes fell, and resultant economies on the GSR's part marked the end of rail communication as far as MGWR western outposts were concerned, *eg* Killala, Clifden and Achill. Similar cuts after World War II forced the closure of the Ballinrobe branch in December 1959, and four years later a flurry of track-lifting wrote *finis* to the sagas of Edenderry, Clara, Killeshandra, Attboy, Ballaghaderreen and Clonsilla–Navan branches. Fortunately, the original main lines to Galway, Westport and Sligo survive as basic trunks routes in Ireland's modern railway system, so that MGWR memories linger on.

Practically throughout its history, the world of the MGWR revolved round Broadstone, a rather awkward off-central part of Dublin where terminus, locomotive sheds, workshops and operational headquarters exercised their various influences. Broadstone station still stands, though passengers no longer throng its busy platforms.

Right: Former Midland Great Western coaches; *top* six-wheeled third of the last century; *centre* six-wheeled lavatory first of 1906 – note the higher roof profile and the top lights; *bottom* corridor composite of the 1920s. (*G. M. Kichenside*)

Locomotives

The MGWR acquired very few locomotives from amalgamation, and relied in early days on stock provided by such firms as W. Fairbairn & Sons, R. B. Longridge & Co., R. & W. Hawthorn, and the Irish firm of Grendon & Co. 2–2–2s handled most main line work until 1870, when 2–4–0s were introduced. The first half-dozen were built by the Avonside Engineering Co, while over the following decade further lots followed from Neilson, Dübs and Beyer Peacock. By this time 0–6–0 goods locomotives had been introduced by M. Atock, Locomotive Superintendent 1872–1901, and initial batches were supplied by R. Stephenson and Avonside in 1876 and 1880. The Standard Goods, as they came to be known, played a prominent role in MGWR locomotive policy, as can be seen from figures which follow. From 1879 onwards, production commenced seriously at Broadstone Works, and subsequent output there kept comfortable pace with 75% of the company's modest, but precise, locomotive requirements. The sheer simplicity of the MGWR range of types made its locomotives a most acceptable complement to GSR stock in November 1924. The valiant service they subsequently rendered was ill-rewarded, for all perished before Ireland's railway preservation movement got into its stride.

MGWR Locomotives Taken into GSR Stock – 1 January 1925

Type	Built	Date	Remarks	GSR Nos	GSR Class
4–4–0	Broadstone	1900–01	'Achill Bogies'. Rebuilt from Beyer 2–4–0s	530–535	D16
	Broadstone	1910–15	Nominal rebuilds from 2–4–0	536–539	D7
	Broadstone	1910–15	Nominal rebuilds from 2–4–0	540–544	D6
	Broadstone	1902–05	Cusack's 'Celtic' class Largest Irish 4–4–0s of their time	545–550	D5
0–6–0T	Kitson/Sharp	1891–93	Small version for local passenger work	551–562	J26
0–6–0	Broadstone	1879–80	First standard goods	563–568	J16
	Broadstone	1885–95	Includes four built by Stephenson	568–579	J18
	Kitson	1901	Bought from WL&WR in 1901	580–581	J17
	Sharp/Kitson	1876–95		582–593	J18
	Broadstone	1885–95		594–613	J19
0–6–0T	Broadstone	1881–90	Heavy shunting tanks	614–618	J10
0–6–0	Avonside	1881	Built originally for the WD&LR	619–622	J6
	Broadstone	1921–24	Final MGWR products Never given names	623–645	J5
	Broadstone	1904		646–649	J2
2–4–0	Broadstone	1889–98	Long lived. Superheated, with 5ft 8in driving wheels	650–668	G2

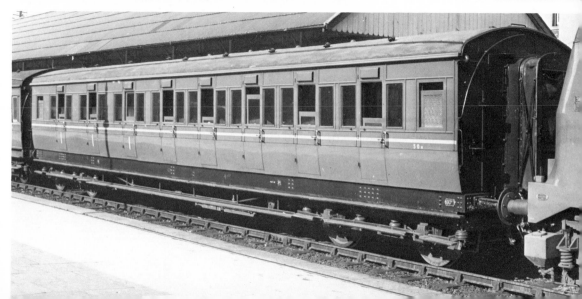

CHAPTER FOUR

WATERFORD & TRAMORE RAILWAY

Incorporated: 24 July 1851   *Opened:* 5 September 1853
Absorbed by Great Southern Railways: 1 January 1925

The Gaelic phrase *Traigh Mhor* means the 'great strand', and it was undoubtedly the attractions of Tramore as a seaside resort which prompted the inhabitants of Waterford to promote the W&TR, after earlier attempts to construct a Cork & Waterford Railway, with its promised branch to Tramore, had failed. £48,000 was duly subscribed, William Dargan was given the contract, and two years later the $7\frac{1}{4}$-mile line, 5ft 3in gauge, was ready for use. Single-tracked and devoid of intermediate stations, it began south of the River Suir at Waterford Manor station, where locomotive sheds and workshops were also located; crossing easy terrain, it ended in a station of remarkably similar appearance at Tramore. The 'one engine in steam' practice adopted by the W&TR obviated the need for signals along the line. Efforts were made later to link up with Dunmore (1853) and Passage East (1862). These

proved abortive, as did a scheme to connect Waterford Manor with stations north of the river, and for the whole of its long life the W&TR remained uniquely isolated from all other Irish railways.

Unlike those of many an other Irish railway, sponsors of the W&TR were well rewarded. Two days after opening 5,000 passengers crowded onto its trains, and such was its continuing prosperity that the W&TR rapidly became something of a legend in Waterford. Never lavish in paying wages, and certainly more frugal than most in rolling stock outlay, it nevertheless contrived to absorb whatever pressures the public cared to exert upon it. In the peak of summer these could be well nigh intolerable. Race days and public holidays saw normal inhibitions simply shrugged aside; most available stock was gathered into one long train, and two locomotives were set at its head. In earlier

Left: Waterford & Tramore locomotives never ran bunker first. On 9 June 1934 2–2–2WT No 483 (W&TR No 1 of 1855) proceeds to the turntable at Waterford Manor station, after which it will again head its train of ex-Clayton coaches towards Tramore. Withdrawn after derailment at Farriglog Bridge in August 1935, and believed scrapped in error, No 483 was one of few single-wheelers in use anywhere at the time. (*T. Middlemass*)

Above: When six steam railcars, Nos 358–363, were delivered to the GSR by Clayton of Lincoln in 1928 they worked for a while on Harcourt Street and Westland Row suburban services, with little success. Heavy on coal, the vertical-boiler locomotive portions were removed in 1932 and the cars, articulated in pairs, were sent to the Waterford & Tramore section the following year. There they proved of great value. Two pairs, with No 360, nearest the camera, are seen at Waterford Manor in May 1934. (*T. Middlemass*)

crises, open wagons hurriedly furnished with temporary wooden seats, were also known to have been pressed into service.

Despite seasonal excitements the W&TR never forgot its local customers. Monopoly or no, fares remained reasonable at all times. Company disciplines, unhurried but quite meticulous, earned local respect, as did the grave demeanour of those who exercised them. Departure of a train involved quite a ritual. Five minutes before the event the station bell was tolled. Tickets were then examined, and each compartment was locked, so to remain until the last moment. This ceremony complete, the bell was rung a second time, platform gates were closed, and after solemn collusion between guard and driver, off trundled the train. It says much for the simplicity of operating technique that only one life was lost during the W&TR's lengthy career, when a train

crashed through Waterford Manor's rear wall on 9 August 1858. Almost 80 years elapsed before a subsequent derailment at Farriglog Bridge brought further injuries, and only those inflicted on the locomotive proved fatal. Then on one memorable occasion, 4 August 1947, history chose to repeat itself, when a GSR 0–6–0T finished up on the roadway behind Tramore station wall. Fortunately couplings broke, so neither coaches nor their occupants were seriously incommoded.

When World War I exercised its grave effect on Irish railways the W&TR's experience proved no exception. Even though spared the subsequent agony of the 'Troubles' post-war deterioration in W&TR profit margins was such there can be no doubt that inclusion in the 1925 GSR amalgamation prolonged the little line's life. By 1931 local bus competition constituted such a threat that local inhabitants, anxious to save their railway, addressed a petition to high quarters. Fortunately, the GSR was able to buy out the offending bus concern. March 1933 saw the arrival of six Clayton coaches. Locomotive portions removed, and articulated in pairs, they proved valuable in handling heavy summer traffic.

Deep shadows fell as the GSR was merged into the CIE in 1945. Miraculously, the W&TR contrived to celebrate its centenary of public service in 1953. Despite warm local response the following winter saw the inevitable, and steam traction was replaced by diesel railcars. By 1960, as in Britain, the CIE was driven to extreme economies; despite strong local protest, the W&TR was condemned. The day the axe fell a feared overflow of Tramore sentiment was discreetly avoided when buses were quietly substituted for the last few scheduled trains. Life in Tramore, it is still felt, will never be the same again.

Locomotives

Was ever a railway more prudent in its employment of locomotives? The W&TR, during its century-long career, bought precisely four! Dargan, in building the line, introduced three ancient 2–2–2WTs of Bury design. These had once run as 2–2–0 tender locomotives on the London & Birmingham Railway. Two vanished immediately the W&TR bought its first locomotives, but one was retained to serve as an elderly No 4 until withdrawn in 1906. When amalgamation took place in 1925 four locomotives and 21 coaches of astonishing variety were handed over to the GSR.

On the occasion of No 3's withdrawal the GSR provided No 560, an ex-MGWR 0–6–0T. So satisfactory was its service at Waterford that as Nos 1 and 4 were scrapped they too were replaced by 0–6–0Ts Nos 555 and 553. All three tanks reached Waterford Manor in similar fashion; they were deposited in an unused siding at Waterford South station, then steamed along sections of rail laid along $1\frac{3}{4}$ miles of public highway. With cabs and footsteps altered to meet restricted W&TR clearances, the 0–6–0Ts served until railcars took over in 1954. Removed from Waterford in August 1955, Nos 553 and 555 were scrapped. No 560 moved on elsewhere.

What other railway could possibly hope to match the W&TR's remarkable tradition of continuity in locomotives and rolling stock?

W&TR	Type	Built	Date	Works No.	GSR No	Withdrawn
1	2–2–2WT	Fairbairn	1855	55	483	1935
2	2–2–2WT	Fairbairn	1855	56	(484)	1926
3	0–4–2WT	Slaughter Gruning	1861	452	(485)	1930
4	0–4–2T	Barclay	1908	1137	486	1941

CHAPTER FIVE

CORK, BANDON & SOUTH COAST RAILWAY

Incorporated: August 1845   *Opened:* 1 August 1849
Absorbed by Great Southern Railway: 12 November 1924

Although most of Ireland's effective early pioneering came from the east, at least two railways in its comparatively isolated south-western corner anticipated the needs of Cork some time before that city was placed in direct communication with Dublin. Both were granted Royal Assent in 1845. One, the Cork, Blackrock & Passage Railway, though launched on a standard gauge basis, reverted latterly to 3ft 0in. The other was the Cork & Bandon Railway, which opened with a modest $6\frac{1}{2}$-mile section from Bandon to Ballinhassig in 1849. The following year a government loan of £35,000 enabled it to push on another $13\frac{1}{4}$ miles into Cork itself. For a short time, pending completion of a tunnel, a service of coaches took passengers into Cork; but by December 1851 the completed 20-mile section was ready for traffic. Taking advantage of the C&BR's presence at Kinsale Junction, one more company, the Cork & Kinsale Junction (1859), blazed its own 11-mile trail to the south coast. The line to Kinsale, an important fishing port, was

Above: Looking very similar in appearance to Beattie's 0–6–0STs for the LSWR, and one of six supplied to the Cork & Bandon by Beyer, Peacock during 1881–94, No 472, classified J24 by the GSR, worked on until 1940. The photograph was taken in 1931. (*L&GRP*)

Below: One year after this picture was taken at Drimoleague Junction in June 1935 4–4–2 tank No 480 was withdrawn, and Class C6 ceased to exist. It and three others were rebuilds, in 1891–94, of older Cork & Bandon 4–4–0 tanks. (*T. Middlemass*)

No 466 was one of eight standard CB&SCR 4–6–0Ts contributed by Beyer Peacock at intervals between 1906 and 1920. The 4–6–0 wheel arrangement was unusual for tank engines in the British Isles. Five lasted until the CBSCR section closed in March 1961, then moved elsewhere on CIE. No 466, fitted with a Belpaire firebox, is seen still active at Skibbereen in 1957, though by then the main CBSCR line between Cork and Bantry was being worked by diesel-multiple-units. (*J. L. Stevenson*)

opened in June 1863, and was worked at all times by the C&BR.

Subsequent moves were westward. In June 1866 the West Cork Railway (1860) linked Bandon with Dunmanway, $17\frac{3}{4}$ miles distant, while the Ilen Valley Railway (1872), backed by £10,000 subscription from the C&BR, carried the line on another 16 miles into Skibbereen. Piecemeal development of this nature was bound to court rationalisation and, surely enough, in 1880 C&BR acquired powers to purchase both West Cork and the Cork & Kinsale railways. A lease was also secured over Ilen Valley metals, but though it had been operated from inception by the C&BR, the Ilen Valley chose to remain independent until 1909.

With the new régime came more activity. In 1881 a further branch of $12\frac{1}{4}$ miles reached out from Drimoleague to Bantry, and five years later nine miles of track were completed between Clonakilty Junction and Clonakilty itself. Almost immediately the latter formed a convenient launching pad for yet another of Ireland's indefatigable light railways. In 1888 the C&BR saw fit to change its name to the more representative one of Cork, Bandon & South Coast Railway. Finally, aided by Treasury interest-free grant, an 8-mile extension was opened in 1893 between Skibbereen and Baltimore. Sponsored initially by the Baltimore Extension Railway, it

was worked by the CB&SCR, which now had continuous main line access of $61\frac{3}{4}$ miles.

The CB&SCR gained a certain amount of prestige when it successfully resisted a railway strike in January 1898, but as the twentieth century opened it was living on pretty thin kale. Local passenger custom was volatile in nature, and only heavy fish traffic between Kinsale and Bantry, plus seasonal tourist activity, kept the company in reasonable shape. Certainly the CB&SCR enterprise did not lack diversity. Bantry's good fortune in being a railhead for the celebrated *Prince of Wales* coach route to Killarney was thoroughly exploited. Equally opportunely, a Bill was obtained in 1900 whose varied contents not only authorised construction of an aerial railway at Ballinhassig to facilitate the transit of locally-made bricks, but also entitled the CB&SCR to subscribe to the Bantry Bay Steamship Company. Active as ever in 1921, the CB&SCR joined a consortium which then proceeded to link its Albert Quay terminus with the GS&WR Glanmire Road station across the River Lee. In the event such benefits as accrued were hardly commensurate with the expense involved.

In common with other Irish railways the CB&SCR was highly vulnerable to problems created by World War I. As part of £2$\frac{1}{2}$ million compensation paid out by the government after years of wartime control the CB&SCR was awarded £75,287; that soon vanished in face of intense post-war road competition – hence, no doubt, the board's ready response in 1922 when the GS&WR invited amalgamation. Held back initially by government intervention, the two concerns inevitably came together again when, as a deliberate consequence of national policy, the Great Southern Railway was formed in November 1924.

Locomotives

Early CB&SCR locomotive history included the use of tender engines, but by 1880 company policy was to employ tank locomotives only, whence Beyer Peacock became the main suppliers. Unusual exceptions were two 0–6–2ST supplied by Baldwin of the USA in 1900, at a time when

British manufacturers were so busy that even several major English companies found themselves obliged to seek 2–6–0 tender locomotives from US sources. The Irish saddletanks were unmistakably American in appearance. The local populace took unkindly to their mournful hooters. Like their American contemporaries in England, their working lives hardly exceeded ten years. Probably in the spirit of 'all hands on deck' the CB&SCR's Cork workshops at Rocksavage produced one 4–4–0T in 1901, but subsequent locomotive construction was again entrusted to Beyer Peacock, whose final contribution, spread over 1906–20, was eight excellent 4–6–0Ts.

The CB&SCR contributed 20 tank locomotives to the 1925 amalgamation, and all were renumbered by the GSR.

Type	Built by	Date	GSR No	Withdrawn
2–4–0T	Dübs & Co	1874	482	1930
4–4–0T	Dübs & Co	1875	477	1930
4–4–0T	Rocksavage	1901	478	1934
4–4–2T	Dübs & Co	1891–94	479–481	1936
4–6–0T	Beyer Peacock	1906–20	463–470	1965
4–6–0T	Dübs & Co (Rebuild)	1906	471	1933
0–6–0ST	Beyer Peacock	1881–94	472–476	1940

CHAPTER SIX
CORK & MACROOM DIRECT RAILWAY

Incorporated: 1 August 1861   *Opened:* 12 May 1866
Absorbed by Great Southern Railways: 1 January 1925

Built to serve a fertile agricultural region west of Cork, and ultimate victor of three competing schemes, the Cork & Macroom exercised what seemed at the time to be prudent judgment by opting to join the Cork & Bandon in the latter's use of Albert Quay as a Cork terminus. Thence, after running on borrowed powers for a mile as far as Ballyphephane Junction, C&MDR trains turned off independently for Macroom, a small country town with a population of 2,000. The initial capital of £120,000, expended reasonably at £6,000 per mile, permitted construction of five intermediate stations along its 24½-mile length. Eventually disputes began to arise over C&BR toll charges and priority of trains. In September 1879 the Macroom railway adopted the rather drastic

remedy of opening up its own new terminus at Capwell, a safe distance from the 'enemy'. This involved disengagement from C&BR tracks at Ballyphephane and construction of a new line into Cork. Despite this considerable expense the C&MDR sought and obtained an additional Act the following year, authorising extension from Macroom to Kenmare. Not surprisingly the extension was never built, and it fell to the GS&WR's lot, backed by government grant, to place Kenmare on the railway map, a few days before it opened the line to Valentia in 1893.

A somewhat similar rebuff attended Macroom aspirations in the mid-1880s, when the narrow-gauge Cork & Muskerry Railway announced proposals to build a branch to Coachford. The

C&MDR's immediate response was to draw up plans for a branch of its own from Kilrea to Coachford. Muskerry opposition proved too strong on this occasion and again Macroom's expansion was foiled. Cork railways seemed particularly prone to this kind of in-fighting, and it was probably no accident that even in 1900 five different railway systems still survived to serve Cork's 80,000 inhabitants. Each had its own terminus, but none was physically connected to any other!

On the other hand the very warmth of Cork partisanship was largely responsible for the C&MDR's early and continuing prosperity. Opened with great public acclaim in 1866, the line carried 81,763 passengers in its first half-year. Receipts were £6,854, and doubtless it was continuation of this satisfactory state of affairs into the 1870s which emboldened the C&MDR to tilt its cap at the Cork & Bandon.

Pride in this instance went before a fall. On 8 September 1878, less than a year before Capwell was due to open, C&MDR triumphal progress was halted by a violent blow from Fate. A train was proceeding smartly towards Cork that day when, a mile or so east of Ballincollig, the locomotive suddenly ripped up a length of track. The subsequent derailment killed driver, fireman and three passengers. The first fatal accident in County Cork, it certainly succeeded in stunning the local populace. Macroom management was placed in a particularly uncomfortable position, for only a few weeks earlier a shareholder had objected to reserve funds being raided to pay a dividend when in his view the money would have been better spent on repairing track. The chairman had ample cause to regret his soothing reassurance that on a simple line such as the C&MDR collision was 'well nigh impossible'. Worse followed when a verdict of manslaughter returned at the inquest saw warrants issued for the arrest of nine directors. Only high-level intervention from Dublin contrived to have the charges withdrawn. It took many years before the incident was lived down, and the drain on company resources in the way of compensation, legal costs etc amounted to nearly £15,000.

Though no dividend was paid for 11 years after the accident the C&MDR's traffic and prosperity increased. All through the early years of the 20th century a 5% dividend was consistently produced. The line gained great popularity with tourists, despite the C&MDR's state of complete separation from other lines. Periodically the matter of re-union with Cork & Bandon tracks cropped up at shareholders' meetings, but Macroom management remained stubbornly hostile to the idea. This remarkable state of affairs persisted right up to 1914 when, in obedience to government dictate, a siding was introduced on CB&SCR territory to facilitate traffic transfer between the two companies. Even then Macroom locomotives were not allowed to run into Albert Quay, wagons being left at Ballyphephane siding to be collected. Immediately the first world war ended the junction was severed, and not until the C&MDR merged into the 1925 grouping was the old link restored, and Capwell's career brought to a close.

Closed down perforce during the Civil War, with damage later repaired by government aid, the C&MDR was probably quite glad to reach the haven of amalgamation on 1 January 1925. As it transpired, shelter under the GSR umbrella brought curiously little comfort. In post-World War I years, railways in the vicinity of Cork suffered more acutely than most. Road competition gradually tightened its stranglehold, and passenger traffic on the C&MDR section withered away, to be terminated officially on 12 July 1935. Such traffic as was left pottered on until the final axe descended, a last goods train running on 10 November 1953.

Locomotives

In the early 1930s five up and four down passenger trains still ran daily on the Macroom section of the GSR. Much stock was second-hand, 1896 being the last occasion on which coaches had been built for the C&MDR. They were in fact the company's only bogie coaches. In keeping with its thrifty existence the C&MDR employed only six locomotives during its lifetime, and five were handed over to the GSR in 1925, together with 27 coaches and 117 wagons. Three were Dübs 2–4–0Ts of early vintage; another was an 0–6–2T built by Barclay in 1905. The history of the fifth is rather more involved; built by Vulcan Foundry in 1921 for the WL&WR, and there named *Derry Castle*, it was transferred to the GS&WR with all other stock when amalgamation was effected in 1901. Purchased by the Cork & Macroom in 1914, it became its No 6. The GSR allotted Nos 487–491 to the five C&MDR locomotives that it inherited, and none lasted beyond 1935.

Above: Quite a history lies behind the 2–4–2 tank seen here at Rocksavage in August 1931. Originally WLWR No 13 *Derry Castle*, it became GSWR No 266, was sold to the Cork & Macroom in 1914, and after Grouping wound-up as GSR No 491R, R being the GSR's Cork & Macroom suffix. The locomotive was withdrawn in 1934. (*L&GRP*)

Below: Cork & Macroom carriages, seen at Inchicore in May 1936. The left hand one is still oil-lit. (*L&GRP*)

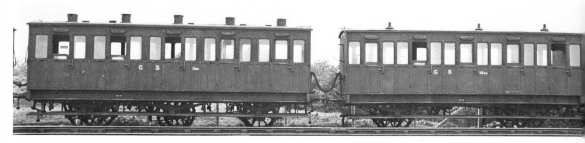

CHAPTER SEVEN
TIMOLEAGUE & COURTMACSHERRY EXTENSION LIGHT RAILWAY

Incorporated: October 1888   *Opened:* 21 April 1891
Absorbed by Great Southern Railways: 1 January 1925

Although by far the smallest standard gauge railway to be found in the Cork area, the T&CELR, Irish to the backbone, still required several Acts of Parliament to stitch itself together. Construction under provisions of the Tramways Act 1883 was completed by 1891, whence the project passed into the jurisdiction of a Committee of Management appointed by County Cork. Despite this, one notes with tongue in cheek that a Vice-Regal Commission, when compiling its report of 1910, seemed less than satisfied with the state of play:

Original rolling stock was so insufficient that a new engine and sixteen wagons had to be supplied out of revenue immediately after the line opened.

The Commission, it might be added, went on to recommend donation of a £5,500 free grant, but only too symptomatic of the times, Westminster took no notice.

It appeared to be a maxim of Irish railway life that whenever the Cork & Bandon Railway created a new branch line lesser bodies were automatically attracted. The opening of its Clonakilty branch was an interesting example of the phenomenon. Vague possibilities now existed of extending rail communication to Timoleague and Courtmacsherry, two small fishing resorts further round the coast. Cork Bandon & South Coast was not particularly interested, but visualising ready-made branch facilities at Ballinscarthy Junction, two minor companies soon sprang up, to

Above: All three locomotives used by the TCELR were tanks supplied by Hunslet. Inside-cylinder 2–6–0 tanks were very rare but *Argadeen*, built 1894, was still active when observed at Courtmacsherry in June 1935 (*T. Middlemass*)

Left: Only the lightest locomotives could work the line between Timoleague and Courtmacsherry, and the GSR used three ex-GSWR Class J30 0–6–0 tanks on it for varying periods. Most celebrated of the three, No 90, is seen at Albert Quay, Cork, in 1957. It was withdrawn two years later, and was later placed on exhibition at Mallow station. (*J. L. Stevenson*)

Below: The reason for Cork City Railway's 5mph speed limit is apparent in this view, taken in June 1938 of passenger stock being moved through the streets to the CBSCR. It is headed by C7 4–4–2 tank No 317, a rare sight in Cork streets after World War I. (*T. Middlemass*)

join forces ultimately in creating the necessary nine-mile line. First into action was the Ballinscarthy & Timoleague Junction Light Railway (1888) with a capital of £23,000. Traffic between Clonakilty and Timoleague began on 20 December 1890, and something of the flavour of the Vice-Regal Commission's observations emerges when one reads that gross receipts to June 1891 of £328 were outweighed by expenditure of £1,095.

Close on its heels the Timoleague & Courtmacsherry Extension Light Railway (1898), with capital of £12,000, opened on 21 April 1891. Amalgamation, with joint capital of £35,000, was soon projected, and the later concern assumed responsibility for working the whole line. The result was remarkable for, exercising its rights as a broad gauge tramway, albeit steam-hauled, the three-mile coastal section from Timoleague onwards shared one side of the public highway as it wandered round the Argadeen estuary to reach the quayside at Courtmacsherry. In keeping with tramway regulations each locomotive was fitted with a bell for use along this section. Curves encountered all along the T&CLER's nine route miles were such that the original bogie stock was carefully confined to 30ft in length.

Typical of Cork railways, T&CELR fortunes began to fade after World War I, when road competition got into its stride. Because of the little railway's local importance, the GSR continued to maintain services, helping Timoleague locomotives by employing equally light ex-GS&WR tanks. Regular passenger services continued to 1947, and occasional excursions ventured down the line until the late 1950s. Daily goods trains ran as required but ended in 1960; 20 August 1960 witnessed an enthusiasts' rail outing, hauled by ex-GS&WR 0–6–0T No 90. Built at Inchicore as an 0–6–4T, one of MacDonnell's light locomotives with carriage portion over the trailing bogie, it was rebuilt in 1915 as a side tank, and assisted on the T&CELR until 1954.

Locomotives

For a standard gauge line the T&CELR achieved something of a record by requiring only three locomotives. All were built by Hunslet of Leeds, and bore names, but not numbers.

The two which passed into GSR ownership in 1925 still escaped numbering, and were allowed to keep their names.

Type	Name	Built	Works No	Withdrawn
0–6–0ST	*Slaney*	1885	382	1920
0–4–2T	*St Molaga*	1890	520	1949
2–6–0T	*Argadeen*	1894	611	1957

CHAPTER EIGHT

CORK CITY RAILWAY

Incorporated: *Opened:* 1 January 1912
Absorbed by Great Southern Railways: 1 January 1925

Railways around Cork developed in such fashion that the CB&SCR and C&MDR remained isolated from other Irish lines for many decades, the River Lee being the obstacle. Then in 1888 the Allport Commission recommended construction of a link to facilitate market opportunities for West Cork produce. Twenty years were to elapse before preparations for through traffic between Fishguard and Rosslare created the necessary incentive. The consortium which financed the Cork City project was highly significant: the GWR of England subscribed £75,000, CB&SCR £15,000, Cork Harbour Board found £10,000, and a government grant of £25,000 completed capital costs. The company's office was established at Paddington, and three directors represented the Great Western, while one acted for the Cork, Bandon & South Coast.

The object was to link the GS&WR terminus at Glanmire Road with Albert Quay, and for most of the required ¾-mile the new tracks ran along the streets of Cork. The Lee was crossed on both north and south channels by electrically-operated lift bridges which handled both road and rail, and opportunity was taken to extend quayside railway facilities. All traffic was worked by the GS&WR. Trains were limited to 20 wagons and a speed limit of 5mph was imposed. Hopes were entertained that through passenger traffic would also develop between the GS&WR and CB&SCR, but somehow this never seriously materialised. Goods traffic justified the link's construction, but fell away after the CB&SCR section was closed in 1961. All traffic ceased from April 1976.

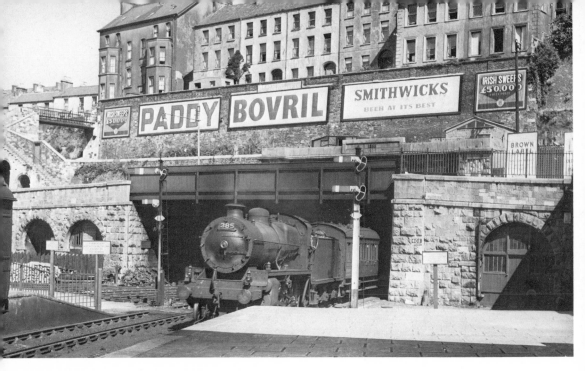

Above: When, after World War I, Woolwich Arsenal relieved unemployment by constructing parts for 100 South Eastern & Chatham type 2–6–0s, 27 sets were bought by Irish railways, 12 by the MGWR, and 15 by the GSR. In the event 26 GSR 2–6–0s emerged; 20, with 5ft 6in wheels, were classified K1, and gave admirable service for the next 30 years. No 385, heading a Rosslare–Cork boat train, arrives at Cork (Glanmire Road) in June 1955. (*G. M. Kichenside*)

Below: Six Woolwich Moguls were fitted with 6ft 0in wheels, as GSR Class K1A, hence the small splashers which can be seen in the picture, as No 397 prepares for duty at Tralee shed in August 1957. (*J. L. Stevenson*)

Right: In 1929 J. R. Bazin, the GSR's first locomotive superintendent, produced five J15A 0–6–0s, an 'improved' version of the GSWR's classic 101s (J15). The new locomotives, Nos 700–704, had larger boilers and weighed $3\frac{1}{2}$ tons more than the originals. Here No 703 is shunting at North Wall in August 1958. (*J. L. Stevenson*)

CHAPTER NINE
GREAT SOUTHERN RAILWAY(S)
Created by Railways (Directorate) Act of 1924
Absorbed by CIE: 1 January 1945

Conditions during World War I saw all Irish railways reduced to desperate straits. By the time the Irish Railway Executive Committee relinquished its wartime control on 15 August 1921 expenditure and minimum wage levels had risen by 300%, whereas income had only doubled. As a consequence maintenance fell into arrears, and provision of new stock became almost an impossibility. The 'Troubles', and indisciplines during the Civil War, caused great interruption of service, and at one stage in 1922 one third of the GS&WR system was inoperative. When things were at their worst the government refused to entertain GS&WR proposals that operations be shut down, as it did a subsequent proposal to merge with the CB&SCR.

Political developments which resulted in the establishment of an Irish Free State focussed urgent attention on the respective merits of (a) amalgamation and (b) nationalisation of all railways within the Free State. Opportunity was

taken by a conference of railway general managers to express a preference for formation of two railways groups, North and South. Unwilling to dally on the issue, the government steamrollered the Railways Act, which became law on July 1924. Under its terms the GS&WR, MGWR and CB&SCR were to amalgamate to become Great Southern Railway. By 1 January 1925 the D&SER was introduced to the fold, absorption of smaller companies commenced, and a new group title of Great Southern Railways was introduced.

With 2,187 route miles (including narrow gauge) under its belt the new company set up headquarters at Kingsbridge, Dublin. As the early 1930s approached rivalry from road vehicles began to bite, but backed by a government much more sympathetically inclined towards railways than its peer in Northern Ireland, the GSR was able to buy or beat off most road competition; inevitably early closing of some more uneconomic railway branches did occur. Much greater

dislocation came the GSR's way during World War II, when acute coal shortage reduced even main line services to a minimum. A similar crisis occurred during the winter of 1946/47, and quite a number of GSR locomotives were converted to burn oil. Peat had already proved unsatisfactory as an alternative. Had not the shadow of ultimate dieselisation already loomed on the horizon further experiment with steam locomotives might have been encouraged.

By this time a Transport Bill passed by the Senate and Dail on 29 November 1944 authorised marriage of all rail, road, water and air transport concerns throughout the 26 counties.

Standard Gauge
Great Southern Railways Locomotive Stock – 1925

	CBSCR	CMDR	TCLR	WTR	DSER	MGWR	GSWR	Totals	Added by GSR (1924–39)
Tender									
4–6–0							17	17	5
2–6–0					2		11	13	26
0–6–0					10	82	135	227	15
4–4–0					5	21	85	111	5
2–4–0					1	19	10	30	—
Totals	—	—	—	—	18	122	258	398	51
Tank									
4–8–0T							2	2	
4–6–0T	9							9	
2–6–2T								0	1
2–6–0T			1					1	
0–6–4T							3	3	
0–6–2T		1					2	3	5
0–6–0T						17	16	33	
0–6–0ST	5							5	
4–4–0T	2							2	
4–4–2T	3				6		14	23	
2–4–2T		1			13		7	21	
2–4–0T	1	3			4			8	
2–2–2WT				2				2	
0–4–4T							17	17	
0–4–2T			1	2				3	
0–4–0T							2	2	3
Totals	20	5	2	4	23	17	63	134	9
GSR Nos allocated	463 –82	487 –91	—	483 –86	422 –62	530 –668			1 to 901
Departmental locomotives					2		10	12	
Railmotors						1		1	

Above: Last of 60 steam locomotives contributed by the GSR were three magnificent three-cylinder 4–6–0s. No 801 *Macha*, in single-chimney form, is seen here at Glanmire Road, Cork in June 1955 waiting to leave with the afternoon mail for Dublin. (*G. M. Kichenside*)

Below: The GSR built five 0–6–2 tanks in 1933, for use on DESR section suburban services. This is No 674, photographed in 1956 at Tara Street station on the City of Dublin Junction line, opened in 1891 to link Westland Row and Amiens Street stations. (*J. L. Stevenson*)

Locomotives Built by Great Southern Railway(s)

No	Type	Class	Running Nos	Built	Withdrawn	Remarks
2	4–6–0	B1	501–502	1924/26	1955/57	Mixed traffic, to GSWR design
20	2–6–0	K1	372–391	1925/29	1955/62	Bought from Woolwich Arsenal
2	0–4–0	M1	280–281	1927	1948	Sentinel shunting locomotives
1	2–6–2T	P1	850	1928	1955	Not a successful prototype
5	0–6–0	J15A	700–704	1929	1955/63	'Improved' J15s
6	2–6–0	K1A	393–398	1930	1955/59	Woolwich Arsenal; with 6ft 0in driving wheels
5	0–6–2T	I3	670–674	1933	1959/62	For DESR suburban services
10	0–6–0	J15B	710–719	1934/35	1959/62	More Improved J15s
5	4–4–0	D4	342–346	1936	1959/60	Built to Coey design of 1907
3	4–6–0	B1A	800–802	1939	1957/64	A fitting finale. No 800 *Maeve* is preserved in Belfast Museum. Largest express locomotives in Ireland.
59						

(A 60th locomotive, Peckett 0–4–0ST No 495, was bought by GSR from Allman & Co of Bandon in 1930 for quayside use in Cork.)

Accordingly, Coras Iompair Eireann was created to perform this task, and on 1 January 1945 all GSR resources passed into its possession.

Locomotives

It is not difficult to imagine the varied collection of locomotives that the GSR inherited from the constituent companies in 1925. Smaller companies bequeathed only tank locomotives, whereas the MGWR and GSWR furnished nearly 90% of the total accumulation. Some of the 581 standard gauge locomotives inherited were promptly withdrawn, but to the GSR's eternal credit those which were taken into stock were most systematically classified, and renumbered where necessary. Despite traditional Crewe affiliations, the system of classification adopted was very similar to that already employed by the LNER in Britain.

New locomotives constructed under GSR auspices in subsequent years were neither great in number nor extravagantly ambitious in design, and four different CMEs served over the years to 1939, when steam locomotive construction in Eire came to an end.

CHAPTER TEN

CORAS IOMPAIR EIREANN

The Transport Company of Ireland came into being on 1 January 1945, when the Great Southern Railways amalgamated with the Dublin United Transport Company, and in so doing anticipated events in Great Britain by three years. All road and rail transport in Eire came under the monopoly of the CIE, except for the area under GNR(I) jurisdiction, which by nature of its dual North and South role still presented unsolved difficulties. CIE was a private concern, with its own board of directors, but the Irish Government, assuming responsibility for guaranteeing debenture interest, reserved itself the right to appoint the chairman. Track taken over, including sidings, totalled $2612\frac{1}{2}$ miles. This figure was later augmented on 1 October 1958, when GNR(I) assets were split between the CIE and UTA. On 1 June 1950 another Transport Act was passed, and the Grand Canal Co was taken over.

Circumstances which forced dieselisation upon British Railways were also present in Eire. By 1950 the average age of the CIE steam locomotives was over 50 years. Many were long overdue for replacement, and World War II conditions, with their chronic shortages, had left most in a poor state. Conversion of a number of locomotives from coal- to oil-burning during the winter of 1946–47, though effective in the short term, also had the effect of dislocating locomotive maintenance. As a result 28% of the CIE total

Above: CIE's first essay into the main line diesel locomotive field was in 1951 when Inchicore works built two locomotives, Nos 1100/1, fitted with Sulzer engines and electric transmission. They were intended for mixed traffic duties and No 1100 is seen here at Mallow on a Dublin–Cork train in 1955. Later the pair were renumbered B113/4 and have since been withdrawn. (*G. M. Kichenside*)

Below: In the middle 1950s CIE embarked on general dieselisation; among the locomotives ordered was a batch of 12 960hp A1A–A1A diesel-electric locomotives built by Birmingham RCW Co with Sulzer engines. The last in revenue service was No 106 here approaching North Wall Dublin with oil tank wagons in August 1977. Others survive in departmental use. (*Michael Baker*)

steam stock was under or awaiting repair. As in Britain, the question of replacing steam by diesel loomed large. The low density of traffic in Eire ruled out on economic grounds the possibility of switching to electrification and the high price of coal in 1950 *vis-a-vis* that of fuel oil tipped the balance in favour of dieselisation.

Replacement was urgent, and in September 1950 AEC received an order for twenty 125hp dmu cars. This was extended to 60 cars in June 1951, while six more, to be built at Inchicore, were ordered in August 1954. The average cost was £18,000 each. Such narrow-gauge lines as remained also received attention in 1951, when Walker Bros and Inchicore combined forces to produce four railcars. Then in 1953 the CIE invited tenders for a fleet of main line diesel locomotives. Three types were specified, and Metro-Vickers featured prominently in their supply. Sixty Type A, 34 Type C, and 19 Type B were purchased. Inchicore shops were remodelled at a cost of £64,000, and by March 31 1958 all diesel units ordered by the Board, except two, were placed in service. Teething troubles were such that a further 39 major units were entrusted to General Motors, of the USA, between the years 1961 and 1966.

As General Motors diesel locomotives were introduced from 1961, all 66 AEC dmu railcars built for CIE during 1951–54 were gradually displaced from main line duties and concentrated on suburban work. Many of them were fitted with bus-type seats similar to those in units built originally for suburban use. Then from 1971 onwards the dmus were converted into push-pull sets, mainly for Dublin suburban service use. Engines were removed and the cars were formed into four-car trailer sets retaining driving controls at the outer end designed to work with re-engined former Class C locomotives now the 201 class. CIE's most powerful diesels, the 071 type, arrived well after the demise of steam, as can be seen from the table below. Diesel classification by letter was dropped in 1972.

The last steam locomotive was withdrawn in 1966, but fortunately six 5ft 3in gauge locomotives from the Republic have been preserved to remind us of former glories.

One last ironic chapter in Irish Railway history was added as this book closed for press when the Irish Republic suffered its worst railway accident on 1 August 1980. The 12-coach 10.00 Dublin to Cork express, behind GM Co-Co diesel-electric locomotive No 075, was derailed at Buttevant, near Mallow. The price paid was 18 killed and 59 injured. A set of hand-worked facing points on the down line, installed for engineering trains to reach a siding, and which had not been connected to the signalbox and thus interlocked, were inadvertently operated by a pointsman in a misunderstanding with the signalman and the express was diverted at 65mph into the siding.

CIE – Diesel Locomotives

Running Nos.	Wheel Arrangement	Built by	Date in service	HP	T/E lbs.	No. of locos	Remarks
101–112	A1A–A1A	Birmingham RCW/ Sulzer/Met. Vickers	1955	960	41,800	12	Used for Departmental purposes only. Originally Type B
401–419	C	Maybach/CIE	1956	400	21,728	19	
421–434	C	Maybach/CIE	1961	400	23,940	14	Similar to 401 Class.
121–135	Bo–Bo	General Motors	1961	950	35,000	15	Versatile Locomotives, whose success permitted withdrawal of steam
141–177	Bo–Bo	General Motors	1962	950	37,500	37	by 1966. (121–35 Single cab, remainder twin cab).
181–192	Bo–Bo	General Motors	1966	1100	37,500	12	Development of 141 Class.
001–060	Co–Co	Met. Vickers/GM/CIE	1968	1325	46,000	60	Rebuild of Type A locomotives of 1958.
201–234	Bo–Bo	Met. Vickers/GM/CIE	1969	1100	34,440	34	Rebuild of Type C locomotives of 1956.
071–088	Co–Co	General Motors	1976	2250	55,100	18	Most powerful Irish diesels.

Preserved steam locomotives from CIE constituents

Type	Class	Number/Name	
2–2–2	—	36	Early GSWR locomotive, built by Bury Curtis & Kennedy in 1845. Displayed at Cork station.
0–6–0T	J30	90	Built in 1875 for Castleisland Railway as an 0–6–4T – combined locomotive and coach. Later, with coach portion removed, it served on the Timoleague & Courtmacsherry section of the GSR. On display at Mallow station.
0–6–0	J15	184	Unrebuilt example of Alexander McDonnell's classic 101 class. Now preserved at Inchicore.
0–6–0	J15	186	Rebuilt, with Belpaire firebox. Preserved by the RPSI, Belfast.
2–6–0	K2	15	GSR No 461. Ex-DSER, preserved at Inchicore.
4–6–0	B1A	800 Maeve	Final GSR steam design. Preserved in Belfast Museum.

Below: CIE's original main line diesel locomotives for principal traffic were the Class A Co-Cos originally built by Metrovick with Crossley diesel engines. Later the locomotives were rebuilt with General Motors engines in which form today they are used on a wide variety of CIE traffic. No 052 is seen passing Howth Junction with a freightliner working on the GN line, while a push and pull train formed of former railcar vehicles leaves the Howth branch on the left on 23 June 1977. (*Kevin Lane*)

Overleaf: Bray station, terminus of the Dublin suburban services on the former Dublin & South Eastern main line. A Rosslare–Dublin Connolly train leaves Bray with General Motors Bo-Bo No B170, of the batch built in 1962, in charge. These locomotives with twin cabs were a development of the original single cab design introduced during the previous year. (*Kevin Lane*)

Above: Rebuilt Class A Co-Co No 022 speeds an express for Dublin Heuston through Kildare on the Cork main line on 22 June 1977. Notice the difference in profile of the BR Mark I type parcels and heating van next to the locomotive, built to the British loading gauge, and the rest of the train of 9ft 6in or wider stock built to the more generous Irish loading gauge. (*Kevin Lane*)

Top right: By the early 1950s CIE had dieselised a number of services with multiple-units, a few years before BR's Modernisation Plan got under way. This is one of CIE's AEC-built diesel motor coaches with first and third class accommodation. During the 1970s many of these cars had their diesel engines removed and worked as push and pull trains in conjunction with rebuilt Class C locomotives on Dublin suburban services. (*G. M. Kichenside*)

Right: CIE buffet car No 2407, part of a batch of coaches 61ft 6in long and 9ft 6in wide built in 1953/4. Prominent is the then CIE emblem, known irreverently and unofficially as the 'flying snail'. (*G. M. Kichenside*)

Left: Normal CIE signals are lower quadrant semaphores but Inchicore up home signal for sighting purposes was at one time formed of a square board with a red stripe to represent a semaphore arm. During the 1970s CIE started resignalling with modern colour-lights and centralised control on parts of the Dublin—Cork main line towards Ballybrophy. (*G. M. Kichenside*)

Right: During the 1970s CIE again turned to British Rail Engineering for new coaches with complete trains of air-conditioned stock, mainly for Dublin—Cork expresses. In dimensions and general appearance they have followed BRs Mark IID and later styles and were finished in CIE's orange and black livery. This is a buffet car which has also served as a State coach. Beyond is one of the 10ft 2in wide coaches built in kit form by Park Royal Vehicles in Britain and assembled at Inchicore. They are of lightweight construction and seat passengers five-a-side in three-plus-two seats on each side of the off centre passageway. (*Michael Baker*)

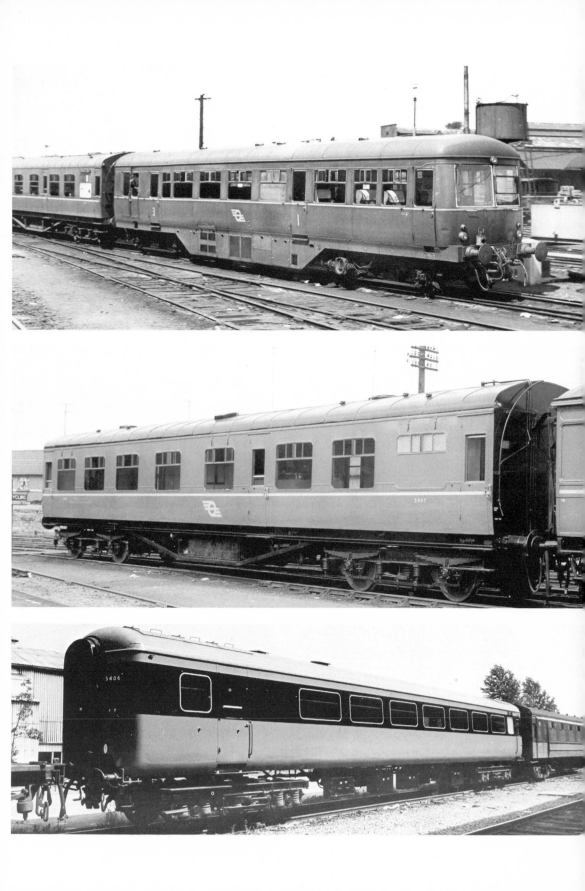

CHAPTER ELEVEN

GREAT NORTHERN RAILWAY COMPANY (IRELAND)

Incorporated: 1 April 1876
Apportioned between UTA and CIE: 1 October 1958

Any railway which succeeded in linking Ireland's two greatest cities must necessarily be of historic importance. Such was the GNR(I). The company itself was not formed until two major railways joined forces on 1 April 1876, but examination of its antecedents takes us much further back – to the year 1835, in fact. Here was an epoch when railway fever, spread from England, was causing Irishmen to dream of more felicitous contact between Dublin and Belfast than the tiresome, and often dangerous, 100-mile ordeal currently offered by horse and coach. By then, too, Ireland's population had swollen to nearly eight millions, nearly twice her present complement. Dublin gazed serenely on as the island's traditional capital, but close on her heels Belfast was thrusting forward rapidly as Ireland's premier industrial centre. Nearby Armagh, bursting at the seams with 500 inhabitants per square mile, had conveniently emerged as Ireland's most densely populated county.

Thus were present all the ingredients required to ignite a positive reaction when one day in November 1835 a group of Belfast merchants met, and resolved to build a railway from Belfast to the town of Armagh, 35 miles south-west. Capital was easily subscribed. Some of it poured in from eager vested interests as far afield as Manchester and Liverpool. Royal Assent was obtained in May 1836, and by March the following year construction was under way. Down in Dublin citizens invited to sponsor a complementary scheme were proving rather less spontaneous in reaction. Subscriptions were sluggish by comparison, and work on a modest Dublin–Portmarnock section of $6\frac{3}{4}$ miles did not begin until July 1838. In the event it took 17 years and the combined efforts of three railway companies, each destined to pass into GNR(I) ownership, before the vital coast route was completed:

Section	Built by	Completed
Belfast–Portadown	Ulster Railway (1836)	1842
Portadown–Drogheda	Dublin & Belfast Junction (1845)	1853
Drogheda–Dublin	Dublin & Drogheda (1836)	1844

Left: The GNR(I) was content to employ four-coupled locomotives for express work. A large all-round version, Class Q, was introduced in 1899, and is shown in this view of No 132 at Amiens Street shed in 1961. Behind No 132 stands No 174 *Carrantuohill* (named after the highest point in Ireland at 3,414ft) an S class locomotive introduced in 1913 to much the same basic design, but with superheater and piston valves. This locomotive, with lightish load, worked the first Belfast–Dublin non-stop run on 26 February 1914, when it covered 112.6 miles in 116 minutes. All five S class locomotives were rebuilt in 1938/39 with long travel valves, and in October 1939 No 174 emerged bearing Dundalk's final Works No 47. Allocated to CIE in 1958, No 174 was repurchased by UTA five years later. (*J. L. Stevenson*)

Above: When GNR(I) and Beyer Peacock introduced their splendid new Class V three-cylinder compounds in 1932 all five were named after birds of prey. They were originally liveried in black and although built with round-top fireboxes Belpaire fireboxes were fitted during 1947–50. No 86 *Peregrine*, UTA-owned by then, is seen setting out from Dundalk in March 1959. No 83 of this class handled Ireland's first *regular* non-stop run of 100 miles when the Enterprise Express was inaugurated in August 1947. (*J. L. Stevenson*)

The Ulster Railway, second in Ireland, was founded (but hardly *opened*, as its company seal proudly proclaimed) in the sixth year of King William IV's reign. By the time its initial $7\frac{1}{2}$-mile section from Belfast to Lisburn was ready for traffic in August 1839 William's niece, Victoria, had already been on the throne two years. Stages to Portadown were completed by 1842. Then, as mentioned earlier, complications arose over the matter of gauge, and in 1849 Ulster's 6ft 2in tracks were reduced to 5ft 3in. This task, costing Ulster £19,246, was more speedily accomplished than was legal collection of the sum that the company was awarded as compensation. No company on whom the levy was imposed was keen to pay, but that hardly excused the Newry & Enniskillen's action in withholding payment of its contribution of £3,997 until 1856!

Carefully and soundly managed the Ulster Railway, though not reaching Armagh until 1848, probed westward to Clones by 1856. Thereafter compromise had to be effected with mushrooming rivals, in course of which the Ulster assumed responsibility for working quite a few minor railways as they were completed. Though always a shade patrician in its attitude toward third-class passengers, the company was at least progressive enough to introduce gas lighting to its coaches in 1865, and for its pains was left sole pioneer in the field for years to come. On 1 January 1876 Ulster's mileage was completed by absorption of Portadown, Dungannon & Omagh (1858), a modest concern whose 27 miles of track it had been operating since 1861.

Ten months earlier, on 1 March 1875, Ulster's two main line rivals had already foreshadowed the coming trend of Irish railway events, when the Dublin & Drogheda and Dublin & Belfast Junction merged to form the Northern Railway Company (Ireland). The combination remained in existence only long enough to absorb the Irish North Western (1862) – formerly known as Dundalk & Enniskillen (1845) – on 1 January 1876 before it, too, succumbed to union with the Ulster Railway. A new name had to be devised – and thus, on 1 April 1876, the Great Northern

Above: The last Irish main line 4–4–0s to be built for the GNR(I) were five Class VS engines supplied by Beyer Peacock in 1948 as a variant on their well-tried Class V Compounds. Simple propulsion, with Walschaerts valve gear, was used in this instance, and the locomotives were named after Irish rivers. Smoke deflectors were also fitted. No 209 *Foyle* backs into Amiens Street in August 1957 to take over a Belfast express. (*J. L. Stevenson*)

Below: When the GNR(I) was formed in 1876 the miscellany of locomotives it inherited included 16 0–6–0s. By the turn of the century, however, the GNR had produced several types of its own. No 11, seen at Drogheda in 1958, belonged to Class PQ of 1899 and, rather intermediate in nature, was styled as power class B. (*J. L. Stevenson*)

Railway Company (Ireland) was born. Subsequent territorial acquisitions and enterprise which were in due course to establish the GNR(I) as Ireland's second largest, and probably liveliest, railway may be summarised as follows:

1877 Acquired Banbridge, Lisburn & Belfast (1858)
Previously worked by the Ulster Railway.

1877 Acquired Banbridge Junction Railway (1858)
Previously worked by the Dublin & Belfast Junction Railway.

1877 Acquired Banbridge Extension Railway (1861)
Went bankrupt after spending £57,300. Bought by the GNR(I) for £3,350 and completed in 1880.

1877 Bought Dungannon & Cookstown (1874)
Originally promoted by the Ulster Railway and Portadown Dungannon & Omagh Railways.

1879 Bought Dublin & Antrim Junction (1861)
Auctioned publicly for £70,000. Previously worked by the Ulster Railway.

1879 Bought Newry & Armagh (1857)
Formerly Newry & Enniskillen (1845). Name changed when the route to Enniskillen failed to materialise.

1883 Bought Londonderry & Enniskillen (1845)
Leased to the Dundalk & Enniskillen in 1860. Thereafter under supervision of the INWR.

1884 Promoted City of Dublin Junction Railway
Opened May 1891 in conjunction with the DW&WR. Made through traffic possible between Kingstown Pier and Belfast, with consequent speeding of English mail to the north of Ireland. Cost born by the DW&WR, GNR(I) and City of Dublin Steam Packet Co. The GS&WR and MGWR declined to assist.

1885 Bought Belfast Central Railway (1864)
Company defeated by street tramway opposition.

1886 Bought Newry, Warrenpoint & Rostrevor (1846)
Opened 1848, but never completed to Rostrevor.

1894 Attempted, with the MGWR, to purchase the Sligo, Leitrim & Northern Counties Railway, but negotiations failed.

1897 Bought Enniskillen, Bundoran & Sligo (1861)
Worked by the INWR from inception, then by the GNR(I) for 15 years. Finally bought for £87,877.

1897 Promoted Hill of Howth tramway
Opened 1901 to stimulate suburban and tourist traffic. Never a financial success.

1906 Part-bought County Donegal Railways Joint Committee
The GNR(I) and Midland Railway of England each acquired half controlling interest in this 3ft 0in gauge railway.

1911 Acquired Castleblayney, Keady & Armagh (1902)
An expensive investment at £350,000, undertaken to keep the MGWR at bay.

GNR(I) affairs prospered until 1914, when rising costs began to outstrip income. Government control over Irish railways was enforced for $4\frac{1}{2}$ years during and after World War I, and compensation was later paid to finance costly renewals of track and rolling stock. Subsequent political 'Troubles' brought both damage and operational problems, for the GNR(I) wandered and looped across the border at no fewer than 17 points. By then small road operators were offering cut-price lorry and bus services, and railways were powerless to compete until 1927. By the time the GNR(I) was able to make a profit from new road activities it was obliged to surrender its road fleet to the Northern Ireland Road Transport Board. Co-ordination promised under this was not forthcoming, and road transport, now under uniform ownership, pressed railways harder than ever.

Influenced by the financial difficulties of 1930 the GNR(I) took an early and effective lead in pioneering diesel railcar services. By 1939 it owned five single cars, four triple units and two railbuses. But by now all Irish railways were facing a desperate economic situation. Second World War years, with their petrol and oil restrictions, brought traffic back on railways, then, as war ended, gloom again descended. In November 1950, with deficits mounting, GNR(I) shareholders demanded that rail operations should cease. Notice was duly given in January 1951 that northern services would terminate from mid-February, but in the interests of maintaining essential public services the government intervened. A joint offer from the North and South governments of £$4\frac{1}{2}$ millions in the way of assistance was accepted, and railway facilities

Above: Atlantic tanks, popular on the GNR(I), were introduced by G. T. Glover in 1913 when five Class T1s were built by Beyer Peacock. No 186 is seen approaching Gormanston, near Drogheda, in August 1958; 20 slightly heavier T2 tanks followed in 1921–29, and both classes saw in the 1960s before their demise. (*J. L. Stevenson*)

Top right: Built for Dublin local passenger services, Class JT 2–4–2T No 94 *Howth* was one of six engines of the class built at Dundalk works between 1895 and 1902. No 93 of this type is preserved in Belfast Museum. (*L&GRP*)

Right: Four Class RT 0–6–4 tanks built by Beyer Peacock in 1908–11 flattered to deceive. Despite their relatively massive appearance they were built for the restricted loading gauge of Belfast Docks, and were less powerful than Clifford's earlier 0–6–2 tanks. All passed to the UTA in 1958, and No 23 is seen here awaiting scrapping. (*T. Middlemass*)

GNR(I) Class U 4–4–0s were introduced in 1915. Built by Beyer Peacock, the class was so successful that five more were added as late as 1948. Two were handed over to the UTA on 1 October 1958; still in fresh GNR livery, No 64 *Lough Gill* is seen here at Strabane on 12 September 1959. (*J. L. Stevenson*)

were kept going a further two years while additional legislation was being considered. Eventually on 1 September 1953 a GNR(I) Board came into being, created by statutes in both Parliaments. Its main requirement, that of being self-supporting, could not be met other than by the exercise of draconian economies. Well aware of this, the GNR(I) Board submitted in November 1954 comprehensive proposals for the closure of minor lines, and replacement of steam by diesel power. Extensive closures from 1955 onwards followed, and a plan to purchase 100 new diesel locomotives never materialised. Even graver events followed on 1 October 1958 when what was left of the once-proud GNR(I) was apportioned equally between two national railway concerns, CIE and UTA.

Locomotives

The miscellany inherited by the GNR(I) from the 1876 amalgamation included five workshops and four locomotive superintendents, and it was decided to centralise heavy locomotive work at new workshops in Dundalk, from where the GNR(I)'s first homebuilt locomotive emerged in June 1887. J. C. Park arrived in 1881 to take

charge, and from his earlier experience at Doncaster with the GNR in England sprang the close resemblance in appearance between locomotives of the two lines. His successors continued the tradition, though, thanks to cramped facilities at Dundalk Works, GNR(I) aspirations never rose above 4–4–0s and 0–6–0s, and even then Beyer Peacock's contribution remained a vital one. Most notable were the small batches of compound and simple 4–4–0s of classes V and VS, some of which were built after the second world war and carried names of birds of prey and rivers respectively. Nevertheless the GNR(I) will be long remembered as a most competent and enterprising concern. Even in the 1950s its express passenger locomotive livery of blue attractively turned out sparkled against the drab blacks and dark greens in Britain and the rest of Ireland. Certainly no other railway contrived, as the GNR(I) did, to operate steam, diesel, electric and horse traction at one and the same time!

Table 3
GNR(I) Motive Power Allocation To CIE & UTA – 1 Oct. 1958

Type	CIE	UTA
4–4–0	28	28
0–6–0	41	38
4–4–2T	12	13
2–4–2T	1	—
0–6–4T	—	4
0–6–2T	1	—
Diesel locomotives	25	28
Totals	108	111

Table 1
Locomotives Acquired by GNR(I) Through Amalgamation

Date of amalgamation	Company	Tender				Tank							Total
		0–6–0	2–4–0	0–4–2	2–2–2	0–6–0	4–4–0	2–4–0	0–4–2	2–2–2	2–2–0	0–4–0	Total
1876	Dublin & Belfast Jcn.	2	3	6	6	—	—	—	—	2	—	—	19
1876	Dublin & Drogheda	1	3	10	6	—	—	—	—	1	—	—	21
1876	Dundalk & Enniskillen	2	1	7	7	—	—	—	—	—	—	—	17
1876	Irish North Western	3	4	1	—	2	—	—	—	—	—	—	10
1876	Ulster Railway	8	10	16	7	—	—	—	—	—	—	—	41
1879	Newry & Armagh	2	—	—	—	—	—	1	2	—	—	1	6
1883	Londonderry & Enniskillen	—	4	—	—	—	—	—	—	—	4	—	8
1886	Belfast Central	—	—	—	—	2	1	1	—	—	—	—	4
1886	Newry, Warrenpoint & Rostrevor	—	—	—	—	—	—	1	—	1	—	—	2
1911	Castleblayney, Keady & Armagh	—	—	—	—	1	—	—	—	—	—	1	2
	Totals	18	25	40	26	5	1	3	2	4	4	2	130

Ulster Railway locomotives became GNR(I) Nos. 101–141, and all other constituent companies' locomotives were numbered under 100. Ten lived on into the 1930s, and the last was withdrawn in 1950.

Table 2
GNR(I) Locomotives Built 1875–1948

	Dundalk Shops	Beyer Peacock	Sharp Stewart	Neilson & Co	North British	Nasmyth Wilson	Hawthorn Leslie	Robert Stephenson	Manning Wardle	Totals
Tender 0–6–0	17	50	9	3	13	11	—	—	—	103
4–4–0	6	66	—	9	9	—	—	—	—	90
2–4–0	—	12	—	—	—	—	—	—	—	12
4–2–2	—	2	—	—	—	—	—	—	—	2
Tank 0–6–4T	—	4	—	—	—	—	—	—	—	4
0–6–2T	—	—	—	—	—	—	—	4	—	4
0–6–0T	—	—	—	—	—	—	1	—	—	1
4–4–2T	—	15	—	—	—	10	—	—	—	25
4–4–0T	10	3	—	—	—	—	—	—	—	13
2–4–2T	6	—	—	—	—	—	—	—	—	6
0–4–0T	—	—	—	—	3	—	—	—	4	7
Totals	39	152	9	12	25	21	1	4	4	267

Top left: Fintona's horse-drawn tramcar, No 381, placed in service in 1893, worked on until the line closed in September 1957. Originally tri-composite, it seated 24 third-class passengers on top, while 24 first- and second-class luxuriated below. This interesting relic of GNR enterprise now rests in Belfast Transport Museum. (*J. L. Stevenson*)

Left: Having climbed to 407ft above sea level to reach Howth Summit, GNR Hill of Howth Tramway cars Nos 4 and 7 prepare to descend to Howth and Sutton respectively. The view was taken in 1956, and three years later the tramway was closed by CIE. (*J. L. Stevenson*)

Above: Striving for economies in its battle against road competition, the GNR(I) converted a road bus to rail in 1934. Still fitted with pneumatic tyres, but employing Howden-Meredith wheels with steel wheel treads and flanges, it played an important part in retaining branch line traffic. Five others were built for GNR use, and the pioneer is seen here at Enniskillen on 15 July 1937. (*T. Middlemass*)

Top: GNR(I) clerestory third originally built with lavatory accommodation. The panelling and general styling of GNR(I) coaches, particularly around the turn of the century, was very similar to the English GNR.

Above: In 1947–9 GNR(I) bought 17 former LNWR coaches from the LMS and BR to help out in a stock shortage. They included corridor thirds, brake thirds and brake composites, originally built between 1906 and 1912 and of both low elliptical and high roof varieties. This is GN No 479, a 1906 corridor third, formerly LMS No 2774. On the split up of GNR assets in 1958 eight went to CIE and eight to UTA, while one had been withdrawn.

Top right: GNR(I) wooden-bodied corridor brake first, typical of main line stock of the 1920s. Note the sliding door to the luggage compartment.

Centre right: By the mid-1930s GNR(I) was building steel-panelled timber-framed coaches like this open third with doors to alternate seating bays to save space on vestibules. It was an arrangement later used by BR on some outer-suburban stock of the 1950s and 60s.

Right: Although most GNR(I) coaches were painted in mahogany brown livery some coaches carried blue and cream livery either for working in diesel multiple-units or as part of the July 1953 royal train; some blue and cream coaches continued as locomotive-hauled vehicles in the Enterprise service like this corridor first. (*G. M. Kichenside*)

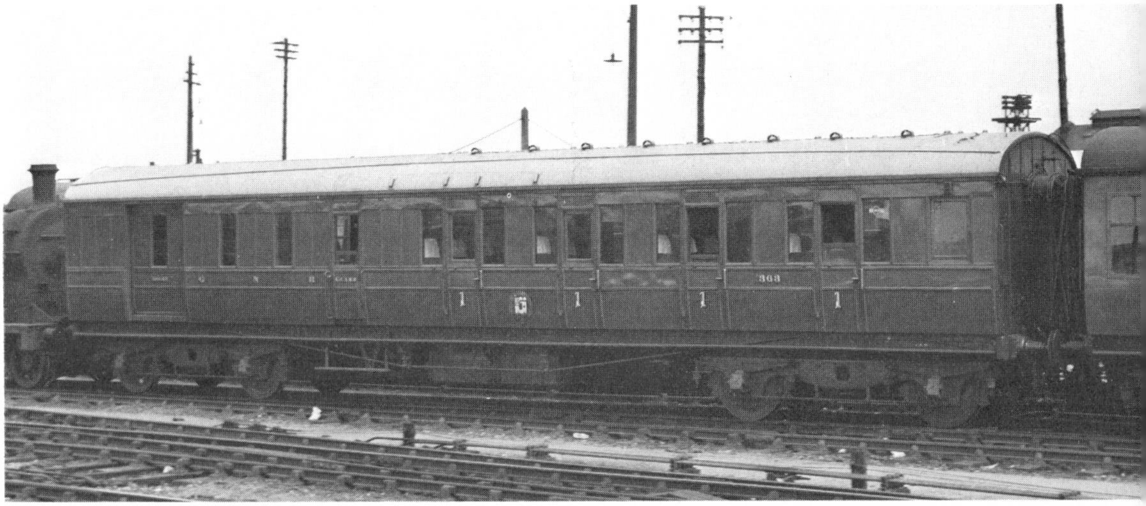

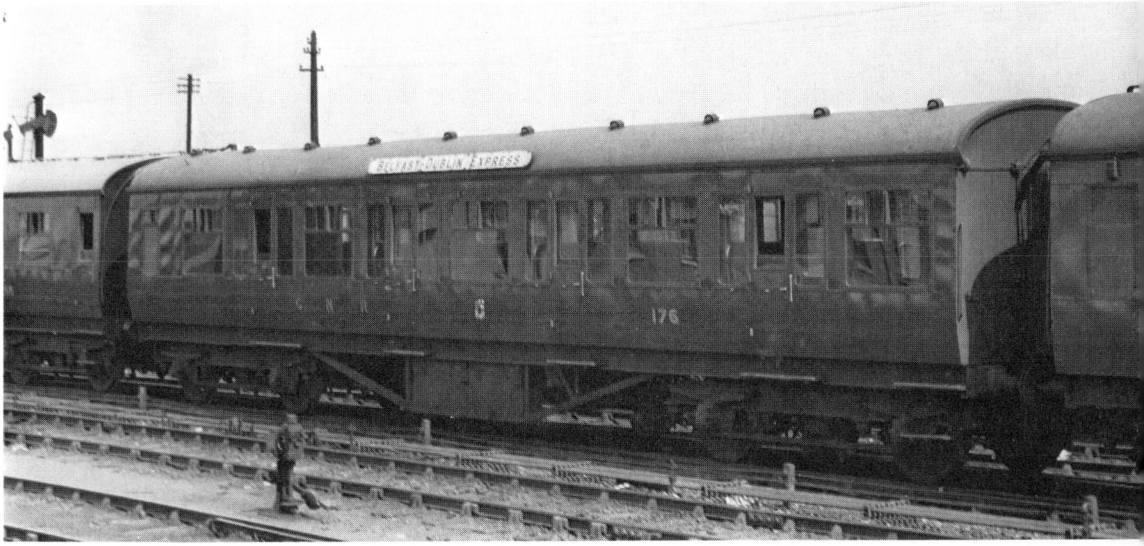
BELFAST-DUBLIN EXPRESS
176

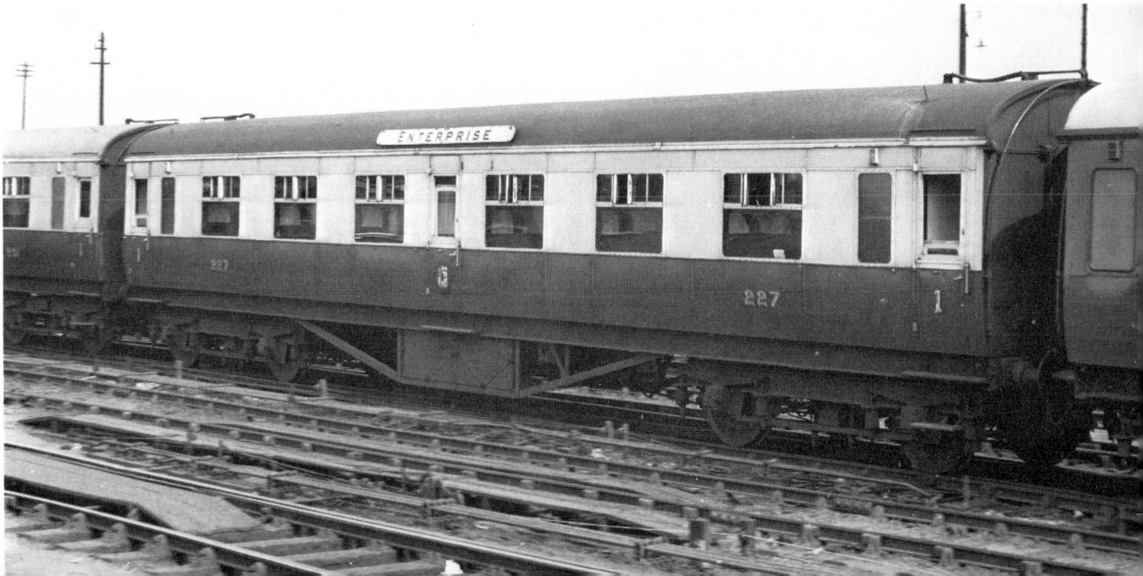
ENTERPRISE
227

CHAPTER TWELVE

DUNDALK NEWRY & GREENORE RAILWAY

Incorporated: 21 July 1863   *Opened:* 1 May 1873
Closed: 31 December 1951

Examine the armorial device of the DN&GR and you will find Britannia clasping hands with Hibernia against a Greenore background of pier, lighthouse and railway, while in the foreground lies an Irish greyhound. The impression this conveys is somewhat misleading, for during the greater part of its existence the DN&GR was, in fact, wholly owned by British transport interests, and despite its separation by miles of open sea it was at all times supplied with rolling stock built in England to the Irish standard gauge of 5ft 3in.

Although the company's origins go back to 1863, the year 1870 holds infinitely more significance in its affairs, for it was then that the LNWR, already operating steamships to Belfast and Kingstown, but ever ready to expand, secured Parliamentary powers to develop a similar cross-channel service between Holyhead and Greenore. Almost a decade before, the Dundalk & Enniskillen Railway (1845), visualising distinct possibilities once a harbour at Greenore had been constructed, had evinced its earnest intention to co-operate by changing its name to Irish North Western. The two North Westerns did eventually come together, but when the critical moment arrived for the INWR to supply rolling stock for the Greenore line financial difficulty intervened and, vanishing from the scene, the INWR wound up in the GNR(I) complex of 1876. One souvenir of its original complicity in Greenore events lived on in the form of a permanent seat on the DN&GR board. Wisely the GNR(I) continued to exercise this privilege well into the 1950s.

Reverting to the early 1860s, when INWR and LNWR collaboration was at its prime, complications arose from an LNWR point of view, when despite ongoing developments, local residents in both Newry and Greenore opted to take matters into their own hands. After some initial compromise each faction put up its own Railway Bill, Westminster duly deliberated, and on 21 July 1863 both Dundalk & Greenore and Newry & Greenore railways received Royal Assent. Sponsoring a railway is one thing, building

it is another. Times were bad in Ireland, and before long both parties found fund-raising such a difficult proposition that little progress, if any, was made over the next five years. The LNWR fretted awhile on the sidelines, then decided in 1864 to throw its own weight behind the D&GR, much to the latter's relief. Straight away a Euston director was seconded to the Irish board, and, laying about it with characteristic gusto, the LNWR proceeded to urge D&GR affairs upwards and ever onward. Traffic arrangements were concluded with adjoining railway concerns, and the Dundalk Steam Packet Company was consulted about future sailings. Ironically, as its involvement deepened, the LNWR appeared to forget a solemn assurance it gave its shareholders in 1862 that participation in a Greenore railway project would *not* involve capital outlay on their part. One wonders how shareholders were pacified years later, when the LNWR found itself obliged to provide not only rolling stock, but steamships as well! Truly, it was an expensive venture.

1867 brought more trouble, when the Newry & Greenore Railway finances suddenly collapsed. Committed to the hilt by now, Euston reacted by increasing its subscription to D&GR funds and nominating Richard Moon as company chairman in 1869. This at least gave the LNWR control over its by now substantial investment. At last, with Moon in the chair, things began to hum. In May 1873 a $13\frac{1}{4}$-mile line from Dundalk to Greenore opened for traffic, and sailings between Greenore and Holyhead commenced. More expense, alas! The packet company previously approached had backed out by now; hence the LNWR had to provide its own ships. Later that year a much strengthened D&GR effected a change of name to Dundalk Newry & Greenore and, taking over the moribund powers of the Newry & Greenore, set to the construction of a $13\frac{1}{2}$-mile section between Newry and Greenore. Once this was opened in August 1876 subsequent contact made with the GNR(I) at Dundalk and Newry enabled the latter to run regular boat trains from Belfast to

Above: DN&GR 0–6–0 saddle tank No 1 *Macrory*, pauses with its three-coach train at Newry in July 1933. (*L&GRP*)

Greenore. With local optimism swelling visibly a new arrival, the Greencastle & Kilkeel Railway & Pier Co, also set itself up in 1876. The intention was to construct a pier at Greencastle, across the Lough from Greenore, and complement its use with $5\frac{1}{2}$ miles of narrow gauge railway. Dissolved four years later, the company never saw its railway line; though the LNWR, once again, did build the pier.

Poor LNWR! The financial consequences of its association with DN&GR must have seemed endless. Ships apart, the INWR defection meant that rolling stock had to be supplied, and uniquely this was done direct from Crewe and Wolverton. Three 0–6–0STs closely akin to Ramsbottom special tanks were shipped across, together with coaches and wagons, for the opening in May 1873. Locomotives were painted black and coaches unashamedly flaunted their own LNWR livery of purple-brown and spilt milk.

Below: A closer look at Dundalk Newry & Greenore third-class coach No 16, with its purple-brown and white livery, confirms its LNWR Wolverton origin (*L&GRP*)

Even with this kind of support it soon became obvious that the LNWR's Irish venture was not to be a success. Ships foundered in the storms of 1881, through rail traffic failed to blossom, and local traffic remained insufficient to reward even a minor railway system. Boldly in the 1890s the LNWR embarked on a policy of modernisation. Automatic brakes were fitted, track was relaid, even new ships were introduced, but by the outbreak of war in 1914 the DN&GR was again failing to pay its way. War itself affected matters little. Partition in 1921 brought prolonged dislocation and damage, for unfortunately the DN&GR bridged both camps, which handicap was later to deny it refuge in the 1925 amalgamation. The end of 1923 saw the DN&GR finish up with a loss of £25,000.

Ownership meanwhile had passed from the LNWR to LMSR, and with six shipping routes now in the latter's possession the DN&GR's prospects looked slimmer than ever. After the General Strike of 1926 passenger sailings between Holyhead and Greenore were not even resumed, while freight and cattle crossings were reduced to three days a week. Two years later negotiations began between the LMSR and GNR(I) with a view to the latter working and maintaining DN&GR services. For a variety of reasons, both political and economic, these took years to conclude, and only on 1 July 1933 did the GNR(I) take over. By then the GNR and DN&GR goods terminals at Dundalk and Newry had been amalgamated. One immediate consequence of the fusion was the transfer of 183 surplus DN&GR vehicles to the LMS NCC section in Northern Ireland. Dundalk meanwhile had been developing the conversion of road buses for rail use, using a patent Howden-Meredith wheel with steel rim outside the tyre. In 1935 two such vehicles were provided for use at Greenore. They proved useful enough in stimulating local traffic, but lack of flexibility in capacity hindered true profitability and in 1948 they were sold back to the GNR(I).

With World War II came fresh shipping problems, and by the end of hostilities the DN&GR was again losing £35,000 a year. In 1942 three of the DN&GR's five locomotives were lent to the NCC to help handle heavy wartime traffic in the Belfast area. Two returned to base in 1944, and the third followed in 1946. It was also during war years 1944 and 1945 that the DN&GR suffered its only accidents, two minor collisions which fortunately produced no casualties.

The creation of the British Transport Commission in 1948 was much more serious, and seemed likely to seal the DN&GR's fate. For a while hopes were entertained that the two Irish governments might combine to rescue Greenore rail services. Alas, these hopes proved groundless, and on 31 December 1951, two days after BTC chose to withdraw its Holyhead–Greenore steamships, the DN&GR ran its last train. Even a blizzard that day did not prevent thousands of well-wishers from turning up to bid the little line farewell. Little time elapsed before all five surviving locomotives were sold for scrap, and an auction at Greenore on 23 April 1952 attended to the disposal of all other assets. Winding up the company, once Abandonment Orders were obtained, posed greater problems than had been envisaged – and it was not until 26 July 1957 that the last trace of LNWR's ill-starred venture vanished from the British courts of law.

Locomotives

Six locomotives, all 0–6–0STs, were built specially to 5ft 3in gauge at Crewe as in the table below.

Macrory was named after A. L. Macrory, a solicitor who played an active role on both D&GR and DN&GR boards. Nos 4 and 5 were built for the Newry extension. No 6, last to be added, was a Crewe rebuild from a DX class 0–6–0. When the line closed *Greenore* was the only locomotive in serviceable condition. Later No 1 was considered for preservation, but in the event only five sets of nameplates were salvaged.

DN&GR No	Name	Built	Works No	Withdrawn	Broken-up at
1	Macrory	1873	1509	1952	Belfast
2	Greenore	1873	1510	1952	Dublin
3	Dundalk	1873	1511	1952	Dublin
4	Newry	1876	1962	1952	Dublin
5	Carlingford	1876	1963	1928	Crewe
6	Holyhead	1898	3877	1952	Dublin

CHAPTER THIRTEEN
SLIGO LEITRIM & NORTHERN COUNTIES RAILWAY

Incorporated: 11 August 1875   *Opened:* 18 March 1879
Closed: 30 September 1957

The name sounds pompous enough, and indeed it reflected the aspirations of those who sponsored this $42\frac{1}{2}$-mile line. Passengers apart, the commercial aim behind its construction was one of stimulating iron and coal mining in the Leitrim area and facilitating the profitable carriage of cattle to northern markets. In practical terms entry into Sligo at the southern end of the line hinged on $5\frac{1}{4}$ miles of running powers over the MGWR, while access north of Enniskillen relied equally on main line connections with the GNR(I). It was in fact withdrawal of the latter lifeline which finally torpedoed the SL&NCR in 1957.

The county town of Fermanagh, Enniskillen had already been reached by rail from both north and east by 1859, and three years later when the MGWR reached up from the south to put Sligo on the railway map no shortage ensued of schemes designed to exploit the intervening area. Nothing came of these until the early 1870s, when a group of influential Sligo citizens resolved to promote the SL&NCR. Financial aid sought under Baronial Guarantee was denied them at an early stage of the Parliamentary Bill, but undaunted they proceeded to raise the requisite £200,000 from private sources. Similar optimism surmounted financial and constructional difficulties met during the building of the first $12\frac{1}{2}$-mile section from

Enniskillen and, almost jauntily, free travel was offered the public on the first day of opening.

Alas, further financial travails lay not far ahead, and the remaining 30 miles to Carricknagat Junction were not completed until 1882. Even then a £100,000 loan had to be obtained from the Ministry of Works which, casting a bleak eye over proceedings to date, promptly and unusually demanded guarantors. Directors and other shareholders duly obliged, and on lurched the SL&NCR into yet another series of financial vissicitudes. By 1890 the Board of Works was so concerned it insisted on having a Receiver appointed. Enquiry produced evidence of operational extravagance, recommendations were made and, duly abjured to mend its ways, the company was left to soldier on. So marginal was any improvement made that by 1894 the Treasury was seriously considering an offer made jointly by

Above: In this view of Manorhamilton shed, taken in July 1933, ex-GNR(I) 0–6–0 *Sligo* features prominently in the foreground. Behind stands SLNCR *Lissadell.* (*L&GRP*)

the MGWR and GNR(I) to purchase the lot for £120,000. The SL&NCR response to this crisis lacked neither courage nor resource. Boldly it applied for release from Board of Works debt, and reduction of loan interest, arguing that if the railway had been constructed a few years later it would undoubtedly have benefited under Tramways & Light Railways legislation of 1883. The ingenious plea worked, for in 1897, after having taken a careful three-year view of the situation, the board finally agreed to financial re-arrangements.

With its burden of loan interest thus reduced the SL&NCR fought its way vigorously into the 1900s, protecting its interests and entering disputes where necessary. Like other Irish railways it suffered grievously when government control produced not only a spate of wage demands in 1917, but a general strike. Then Partition, following-up in 1921 with its artificially determined boundary, brought fresh problems. The Border crossed SL&NCR tracks $\frac{1}{2}$-mile west of Belcoo, and an Imperial Customs post established there in 1923 brought little but additional dislocation and expense as far as the SL&NCR was concerned. Escape into the GSR complex of 1925 was automatically debarred because $12\frac{3}{4}$ miles of track lay inside Northern Ireland. Poor old SL&NCR – who could tell that 30 more weary years lay ahead!

After Partition came the 'Troubles'. Delicately poised on the front line as it were, the Sligo Leitrim suffered accordingly. Even the mercy of a cease fire in 1923 brought little respite, for by now post-war bus competition in the area was growing in menace. Hopes rose in 1932 when a GNR(I) light diesel railcar ran successful trials between Sligo and Enniskillen, producing costs of 3d per mile as opposed to steam's 1s 0d. But even this shaft of light was soon extinguished, for prolonged economic dispute between the two Irish governments, and a railway strike in the North, soon reduced the company to near-bankruptcy; from 1935 onwards only regular receipt of Stormont Grants-in-Aid kept the SL&NCR alive. During World War II rail traffic picked up, thanks to petrol restrictions, and an unexpected bonus emerged when, running short of coal, the Free State diverted a considerable amount of Dublin–Sligo traffic discreetly over the GNR(I) and SL&NCR via Enniskillen. As far as the sensitive area of wartime security was concerned the SL&NCR's somewhat schizophrenic position

Right: Hazlewood was badly damaged during the 'Troubles' of 1923, but still outlived sister locomotives to witness the SL&NCR's closure in 1957. When the company's assets were auctioned in April 1959 efforts to save *Hazlewood* for preservation failed and it, plus *Sir Henry* and *Lough Gill*, went under the hammer for a total sum of £910. *Hazlewood* is seen heading a train out of Enniskillen on 8 August 1956. (*J. L. Stevenson*)

was simply resolved by the removal of station nameboards all down the line!

Post-war years looked promising enough, but the impending impact of inflation was duly felt when a Walker railcar ordered in 1944 at an estimated cost of £8,000 arrived in 1947 priced £10,522. Worse was to follow that year; unable to borrow steam locomotives from either the GNR(I) or CIE, and acting contrary to all established financial principles, the SL&NCR was rash enough to order two new 0–6–4Ts from Beyer Peacock. In the absence of hard cash painful and prolonged negotiations followed. Ultimately resort was made to hire-purchase, and only in 1951 was belated delivery effected. By now the GNR(I) had joined the SL&NCR in such financial straits that *both* Irish governments were obliged to assist. Uneasy years followed. Late 1957 found the government of Eire still prepared to furnish fixed annual subsidies of up to £15,000 to keep the SL&NCR alive. Unfortunately, the Northern Ireland government, traditionally less interested in railways, had already pre-empted the situation by declaring its intention to close, amongst others, the GNR(I) line through Enniskillen. On 30 September 1957 the fatal wound was inflicted, and the SL&NCR ran its last sad train to Sligo. The miracle was, perhaps, that despite a lifetime of combat against adverse financial odds this gallant little railway survived for $78\frac{1}{2}$ years.

Right: Although sold for scrap in 1954, *Lissadell* (complete with nameplates) still lay at Sligo when this photograph was taken in August 1956. (*J. L. Stevenson*)

Locomotives

The SL&NCR owned 20 locomotives in its lifetime, and scrapped none, for all were either sold or auctioned after withdrawal. Some were new when bought, others were secondhand, and no class ever exceeded five in number. Locomotives bore names, but not numbers. Company workshops at Manorhamilton attended to their welfare, and livery adopted was black. The SL&NCR's favourite indulgence was a Beyer Peacock design of 0–6–4T, earlier used by South Australian Railways. The last brace, delivered in such controversial circumstances in 1951, marked the end of (conventional) steam locomotive construction in Ireland.

One last melancholy detail of the SL&NCR story remains to be added. After rail operations ceased in 1957 liquidators were appointed and the entire company assets, rolling stock, stations, bridges etc were auctioned on Northern Irish and Eire sites, on 1 October 1958 and 28/29 April respectively.

New Locomotives Built for SL&NCR

Type	Name	Built by	Works No	Date	Withdrawn	Disposal
0–6–2T	Pioneer	Avonside Eng	1197	1877	1921	1928
	Sligo	Avonside Eng	1198	1877	1921	1928
0–6–4T	Fermanagh	Beyer Peacock	2137	1882	1952	1952
	Leitrim	Beyer Peacock	2138	1882	1947	1952
	Lurganboy	Beyer Peacock	3677	1895	1953	1953
	Lissadell	Beyer Peacock	4073	1899	1954	1954
	Hazlewood	Beyer Peacock	4074	1899	1957	1959
4–4–0T	Erne	Hudswell Clarke		1883	1911	1912
0–6–4T	Sir Henry	Beyer Peacock		1904	1957	1959
	Enniskillen	Beyer Peacock		1905	1957	1959
	Lough Gill	Beyer Peacock		1917	1957	1959
	Lough Melvin	Beyer Peacock		1949	1957	1959
	Lough Erne	Beyer Peacock		1949	1957	1959

Locomotives Purchased Secondhand by SL&NCR

Type	Name	Built by	Date	Withdrawn	Sold
0–4–0ST	Faugh-a-Ballagh	Hunslet	—	1905	1905
0–6–0T	Waterford	Hunslet	1893	1923	1928
4–4–0	Blacklion (a)	Beyer Peacock	1885	1931	1938
	Glencar	Beyer Peacock	1887	1928	1928
0–6–0	Glencar (b)	Beyer Peacock	1890	1949	1949
	Sligo	Beyer Peacock	1890	1941	1941
	Sligo	Beyer Peacock	1882	1949	1949

NOTES:
(a) Purchased from GNR(I) after 0–6–2Ts were withdrawn. Limited use in SL&NCR, being only able to handle light trains. Parts of *Glencar* were ultimately cannibalised to reconstruct *Blacklion* at Dundalk works.
(b) With Beyer Peacock quoting £5,335 for a new tank locomotive in 1937, the SL&NCR opted to persevere with further purchase of tender locomotives. Two GNR(I) 0–6–0s were brought after trials in 1928 and 1931. In 1941 the GNR(I) replaced *Sligo* with another 0–6–0. Two more 0–6–0s were later hired in 1947 and 1950.

Railbuses Purchased by SL&NCR

Letter	Source	To stock	Disposal
A	Ex-GNR(I)	1925	Destroyed in collision, 7 March 1939
2A	Ex-GNR(I)	1938	Auctioned at Enniskillen, 1958
A	Ex-GNR(I) (replacement)	1939	Auctioned at Manorhamilton, 1958
B	Walker Bros	1947	Purchased by CIE, 1958

Above: Lough Erne, one of two Beyer Peacock 0–6–4 tanks surprisingly ordered in 1947 when the SL&NCR was in straitened circumstances, shunts quietly at Enniskillen in August 1957. Still, financially speaking, owned by Beyer Peacock, it and *Lough Melvin* passed into UTA ownership in 1959, whence they acquired numbers 26 and 27. (*J. L. Stevenson*)

Below: Sligo, Leitrim & Northern Counties Railway six-wheel third photographed at Enniskillen in 1933. Internally the compartments are divided into two-compartment divisions with a low back seat in the centre, each lit by a single oil lamp. (*L&GRP*)

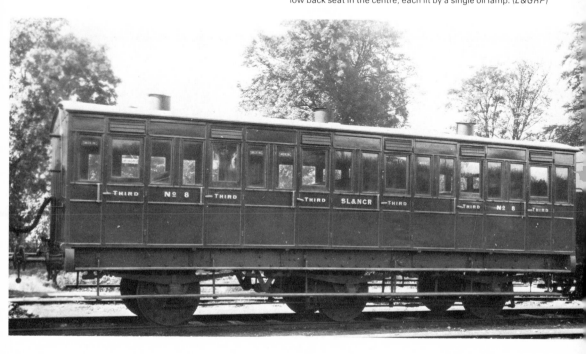

CHAPTER FOURTEEN
BELFAST & COUNTY DOWN RAILWAY

Incorporated: 20 June 1846   *Opened:* 2 August 1848
Absorbed by Ulster Transport Authority: 1 October 1948

Halfway through the 'Railway Mania' of 1845–46 Westminster found itself examining three Irish Bills, each of which purported to offer appropriate railway facilities for County Down. In the ensuing scramble Great County Down's Bill failed to last the course, the Belfast & Hollywood Atmospheric was wheedled (mercifully perhaps!) into withdrawing its application, and the survivor, the Belfast & County Down Railway, emerged endowed with powers to link Belfast with sundry points in the Co Down area. Priority in the view of its sponsors lay in servicing Belfast's rapidly expanding suburbia, and with this aim in sight four miles of single 5ft 3in track to Hollywood were opened in 1848. A complementary 13-mile link with Newtownards followed in 1850, and coastal connection with Donaghadee was established eleven years later. The latter turned out to be a poor investment, for despite provision of a fine new harbour at government expense Donaghadee's significance as a cross-Channel port soon faded in face of competition from Larne.

From its inception it became obvious that the BCDR's welfare was to march hand-in-hand with that of Belfast. By the close of the century the city's population, a mere 30,000 in 1850, had soared to 360,000. Increasing numbers of residents were opting to move further out of town, and railway passenger receipts swelled accordingly. Ready to serve, the BCDR set about expanding its modest monopoly, and subsequent shrewd investments saw its compact network achieve a final total of 80 route miles:

1884 Bought Belfast Hollywood & Bangor (1860)
An important suburban acquisition. Opened between Hollywood and Bangor in 1865, but worked from inception by the BCDR. Six locomotives transferred, and the two companies' adjacent stations at Queen's Quay amalgamated.

1881 Bought Downpatrick Dundrum & Newcastle (1866)

11½ miles long; opened 1869. With this purchase the BCDR was able to move into Newcastle from Downpatrick.

1880 Sponsored Downpatrick Killough & Ardglass Railway
Worked and maintained by the BCDR. Eight miles long, its construction was assisted by Treasury Grant and Baronial Guarantee, as a form of indirect aid to Ardglass' herring industry.

1906 Opened Castlewellan Extension
3½-mile section built to hold GNR(I) ambitions in check. After Arbitration proceedings the two companies traded running powers between Newcastle and Ballyroney, and shared maintenance of Newcastle station.

Thus the year 1906 found the BCDR in very good heart indeed. Freight traffic still formed a minor part of its activity, but given the agricultural nature of much of County Down this was not unacceptable. Meanwhile, steamship and hotel management had been added to BCDR accomplishments, and fruits therefrom enhanced dividends, already healthy in nature, which had rewarded a vigorous board reshuffle in 1875. Clearly as a measure of continuing prosperity, Queen's Quay station was handsomely rebuilt during 1910–14 at a cost of £26,000. Pioneer experiments having been conducted in road transport the company was also proud owner of a modest fleet of steam and petrol wagons. Buses were added in 1916. Then came the Armistice, and the blizzard it released of bus and private car competition soon eroded BCDR confidence. A defensive fare war embarked upon only reduced passenger receipts still further. Still fighting, in 1928 the BCDR systematically bought-out all local bus competition, but even this brave move was largely negated when in 1935 all Northern Ireland railways were obliged by law to hand-over their road stock to the newly-created Northern Ireland Road Transport Board. Any chance to

Above: Between 1892 and 1921 Beyer Peacock built four 0–6–0s for the BCDR. No 14, deemed the Intermediate Class, had the distinction of introducing the BCDR's first Belpaire firebox in 1904. (*T. Middlemass*)

Below: The last locomotive built for the BCDR and supplied by Beyer Peacock in 1945, 4–4–2 tank No 9 saw only 11 years' service before being sold for scrap in 1956. This locomotive's weight of 66 tons restricted its use on the BCDR's comparatively light lines. Beyer Peacock could only supply a new engine at that time by using an existing design, albeit over 20 years old. (*T. Middlemass*)

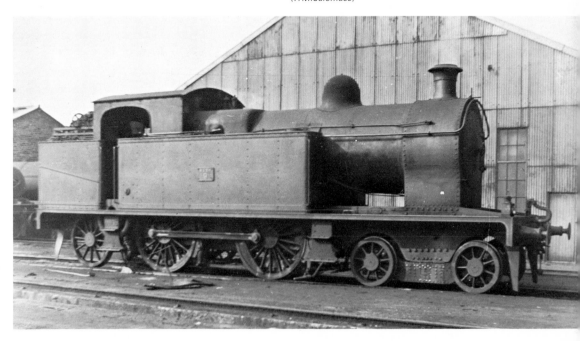

Above: This general view of the BCDR sheds in Belfast, taken in 1931, underlines the company's devotion to Atlantic tanks. (*L&GRP*)

Right: Four massive Baltic tanks supplied by Beyer Peacock in 1920 proved a poor investment for the BCDR. At 81½ tons they were much too heavy for use other than on the Bangor line, and being unsuperheated were heavy on coal. No 24 is seen at Queen's Quay in 1947. All four passed into UTA ownership the following year, and when auctioned for scrap in 1956, three of them fetched £1,170 each. (*L&GRP*)

resolve this fresh imbalance vanished as World War II approached.

When German aircraft bombed Belfast in 1941 BCDR property did not escape their attention. Queen's Quay suffered particularly, but despite that the company played an active role all through the conflict, transporting workers, evacuees and troops alike as circumstances demanded. Then, as before, wartime popularity of rail transport soon faded as private motoring was fully restored. In a drastic attempt to stave off the inevitable the BCDR management even went so far as to place itself under GNR(I) jurisdiction from 1944 onwards. In all other respects the companies retained their separate identities. One GNR(I) triple-unit diesel railcar assisted around Belfast for a while, as did a 2–4–2T borrowed from the GSR.

Typically late in the day, it was 1946 before the government of Northern Ireland steeled itself to grasp the transport nettle. A White Paper postulated amalgamation of all railway lines left in Northern Ireland. The GNR(I)'s continuing dual role north and south of the Border made its immediate inclusion impossible, but NCC, BCDR and NIRTB were duly merged. From 1 October 1948 their combined rolling stocks functioned under the auspices of the Ulster Transport Authority. BCDR shareholders were compensated to the tune of £485,989, just over a century after their first proud train steamed from Belfast to Hollywood.

Locomotives

In 1846, after deliberating over tenders from six different firms, the BCDR elected to buy its first locomotives from Bury Curtis & Kennedy. After that it dabbled with a succession of suppliers, and it was not until the lengthy aegis of R. G. Millar (locomotive superintendent 1890–1919) commenced that some measure of standardisation in locomotive policy began to emerge. Shortly after Millar's accession an 0–4–2 of sorts was built from spare parts at Queen's Quay shops. The experiment was never repeated, and from 1891 onwards all new construction was entrusted to Beyer Peacock of Manchester. It follows that two distinct phases emerge in BCDR locomotive history:

Locomotives Built – 1848–1890

Built by	Type	Date	Number built
Bury Curtis	2–2–2	1848	4
Fairbairn	2–2–2WT	1850–51	2
Fairbairn	0–4–2	1859–83	4
Manning Wardle	2–4–0	1868	2
Vulcan Foundry	2–4–0ST	1864–84	7
Vulcan Foundry	0–6–0	1875	1
Beyer Peacock	2–4–0T	1857–59	3
Beyer Peacock	0–6–0	1878	1
Sharp Stewart	0–4–2	1880–90	5
BCDR	0–4–2	1895	1
Yorkshire Eng Co	2–4–0T	1884	2
		Total	32

Thus of BCDR's total of 73 locomotives 45 emanated from Beyer Peacock's workshops. Like some English contemporaries the BCDR went through a compound phase in the 1890s, but by the turn of the century simplicity again prevailed. Predominance of tank engines thereafter is noteworthy. Tanks, the BCDR found, were admirably suited to fast suburban traffic, and the Atlantic type, first imported from Beyer Peacock in 1901, came to form the backbone of BCDR modern locomotive stock. Latterly this policy rather defeated its own end, for the quartet of massive Baltic tanks introduced in 1920 proved much too heavy for use other than on the Bangor line.

Two serious derailments blemished the BCDR's traffic record. One, a derailment at Ballymacarrett Junction in 1871, brought death to two passengers, and injuries to 55 others. The second, occurring very near the same spot, was a much more sombre affair. A push-pull train ran into the rear of a passenger train on 19 January 1945; on this occasion 23 passengers were killed and 24 injured. Compensation cost the BCDR £75,000.

When BCDR locomotives passed into UTA ownership in 1948 all 29 had 200 added to their running numbers and locomotive repairs now became the exclusive province of York Road shops. Up to 1951 a considerable amount of running was done on the BCDR by NCC 2–6–4Ts and 2–6–0s, but by 1955 branch closures were such that only the Bangor line remained. Of the 23 BCDR locomotives which then survived, four serviceable Atlantic tanks and one 0–6–0 were transferred to the NCC section. With no major repairs being undertaken the remainder were allowed to lie redundant around Queen's Quay shed. Ultimately 4–4–2T No 230 was retrieved for preservation, and six more were sold privately. The rest mouldered on to form the nucleus of a melancholy auction held at Queen's Quay in January 1956. So, on this underservedly subdued note, ended the saga of the Belfast & County Down Railway.

CHAPTER FIFTEEN

NORTHERN COUNTIES COMMITTEE

Title created by Midland Railway: 1 July 1903
Absorbed by UTA: 1 October 1948

When the railway age arrived in Ireland nowhere were its ideals more warmly embraced than in the northern counties of Antrim and Londonderry, for already many engaged in the linen industry had savoured the benefits of the Industrial Revolution. Belfast too was growing at meteoric rate, and a natural instinct to link it by rail with Dublin soon emerged in 1825. It was not translated into practical terms until ten years later when the Ulster Railway was launched, and by then a kindred enthusiasm to press northward had also been generated by prominent Belfast citizens. An initial proposition to connect Belfast with Ballymena was, however, vetoed by a sudden financial slump, and the North-Eastern Railway fell by the wayside. A decade later with the same men at the helm the concept was revived, and the Belfast & Ballymena Railway was given Royal Assent on 21 July 1845. Trains were on the move by April 1848, but so hastily had the line been constructed only passenger traffic could be handled at first.

Further north the city of Londonderry was also stirring. The trade from which it thrived sprang largely from its close connection with the City in London, and it was support from this source which prompted the promotion of two outgoing railways in 1844: one to Strabane and Enniskillen, the other to Coleraine. Both companies were incorporated on the same day, 4 August 1845, and sharing substantially the same board they marched together until 1860, when the Londonderry & Enniskillen was leased to the Dundalk & Enniskillen Railway, and ultimately became part of the GNR(I).

The remaining partner, the Londonderry & Coleraine Railway, launched with such enthusiasm in 1845 soon found that the programme of tunnelling and land reclamation it undertook had been grossly underestimated. A second Act had to be obtained in 1850, allowing five more years for completion; rapidly developing financial difficulties required a third, more ominous, Act in 1852, whereby the original company was dissolved, and new arrangements approved. By December that year passengers were able to travel between Londonderry and a branch at Limavady, and seven months later the 34-mile line was completed to Coleraine. An accident or two which came its way suggested the company was no more gifted in operational procedure than it was in finance. 1853 found bankruptcy looming ahead, and the Board elected to ride the storm by persuading a large creditor to undertake long lease of the line.

By now, with companies reaching north to Ballymena and east to Coleraine, only a gap of 30 miles prevented a through rail link between Londonderry and Belfast. The question of who was to close that gap was resolved on 8 July 1853 when an impressive sounding Ballymena, Ballymoney, Coleraine & Portrush Junction Railway made its debut. The surprising inclusion of Portrush in the title reflected an ambition of the chairman, the Earl of Antrim, to advance the welfare of this seaside resport, which incidentally formed part of his estates. Events were soon to move swiftly. The Belfast & Ballymena changed its title to Belfast & Northern Counties Railway on 15 May 1860, the new company absorbed the Earl of Antrim's railway early in 1861, while, leased since 1860 by the B&NCR, the Londonderry & Coleraine followed suit on 24 July 1871.

The opening of an important bridge across the River Bann at Coleraine in November 1860 enabled the B&NCR to run through trains between Belfast and Londonderry, and set the stage for vigorous expansion. By 1862, well ahead of the times the company was offering third-class travel on all trains, and in October of the same year the opening of the Carrickfergus & Larne Railway (1860) introduced a new short sea crossing of 36 miles to Stranraer.

Many sections of the B&NCR were double-tracked, steel rails were introduced, and harbour facilities were extended over the following two decades, whence acquisition of two more standard

Above: The Belfast & Northern Counties Class C light compound 2–4–0s were supplied by Beyer Peacock between 1890 and 1895. No 57 was rebuilt with 5ft boiler in 1931, reclassified C1, and received the name *Galgorm Castle* from 4–4–0 No 3. The first locomotive in the world to have Ross pop safety-valves (the inventor lived in Coleraine), No 57 was also the only NCC 2–4–0 to carry an LMS-type chimney. It survived until 1938, being photographed at Cookstown in July 1936. (*L&GRP*)

Below: No 55 *Parkmount* commenced life in 1895 as one of the Belfast & Northern Counties two compound Class D 2–4–0s. Their driving wheels, 7ft 0in diameter, were the largest in Ireland. Both were converted to 4–4–0s in 1897, but whereas No 50 *Jubilee* was restored to simple propulsion, *Parkmount* remained a compound until withdrawn in September 1944. The weatherboard on the tender was acquired in 1935. (*T. Middlemass*)

gauge lines (in addition in several narrow-gauge enterprises) rounded off B&NCR progress. This culminated in a standard gauge route mileage of 193 miles.

1895 Acquired Draperstown Railway (1878)
Eight-mile branch between Magherafelt and Draperstown, opened July 1883, worked by the B&NCR. The latter took possession from Board of Works in 1895.

1901 Acquired Derry Central Railway (1875)
29½-mile line joining Magherafelt with Macfin. Opened February 1880 and worked by the B&NCR. After an unfortunate history possession passed to the B&NCR, again via the Board of Works!

Two years later the B&NCR itself was absorbed, when the Midland Railway, anxious to compete with the LNWR and GWR in cross-channel services, constructed a fine new harbour at Heysham and matched it with an equally handsome bid for ownership of the B&NCR. Vesting under Midland Railway auspices was completed on 1 July 1903. One more acquisition, that of the Limavady & Dungiven Railway (1878), followed in August 1907. By now the B&NCR's title had been changed to Northern Counties Committee (Midland Railway). For many years the line retained its old characteristics, and only when Grouping in Britain produced the LMSR,

Above: The building of four Class W 2–6–0s in 1933 marked a clear change of LMS locomotive policy in Northern Ireland. They had 6ft driving wheels and were clearly intended for express duty including the North Atlantic Express between Belfast and Portrush. They showed distinctive affinities with the LMS Crab 2–6–0s and Fowler 2–6–4Ts in Britain. This is No 96 *Silver Jubilee* of a later batch. Some of the 2–6–0s were given outside steampipes. (*L&GRP*)

Top right: Class V 0–6–0 No 15 was one of a superheated trio of NCC engines imported from Derby in 1923. For a few months the locomotives ran as X, Y and Z, before being numbered 13 to 15. When seen in 1956 No 15, complete with Belpaire firebox and flat top dome, looked much more like a standard Midland 0–6–0. (*J. L. Stevenson*)

Right: Class U2 4–4–0 No 81 *Carrickfergus Castle*. This class was evolved from B&NC compound Class A 4–4–0s dating from 1901, some of which were rebuilt as two-cylinder simple expansion engines and gradually Midlandised (Midland in this sense being the English concern which owned the NCC, not the Irish Midland Great Western) as Class U2. The LMS then built 10 new U2s in 1924/5, looking uncannily like the Derby 2P 4–4–0, the LMSR's ultimate contribution to Irish 4–4–0s, which served on the NCC and UTA until 1961. (*L&GRP*)

did the Irish railway become NCC(LMSR) on 1 January 1923, when Midland practice really exerted itself. From thereon crimson-lake livery was adopted for both locomotives and coaching stock. Further British railway developments in January 1948 occasioned a further change of title to Railway Executive, Northern Counties Committee, and creation of the Ulster Transport Authority later that year resulted in the sale of the NCC by British Transport Commission on 1 April 1949 for £2,668,000. Later still, on 1 April 1968, Northern Ireland Railways assumed responsibility.

Locomotives

While the three constituent Companies of the B&NCR contributed a variety of early single-wheeled types, the Belfast & Ballymena was also employing Sharp 2–4–0s by 1856; like the MGWR the B&NCR exercised a fondness for the type almost to the end of the nineteenth century. Only in 1897 were 4–4–0s introduced. Few tank locomotives were ever required, but 0–6–0s found favour as far back as 1870, again built by Sharp Stewart. Enterprising to a degree, the B&NCR

provided itself in 1862 with locomotive sheds and workshops at York Road, Belfast. During that year it also conducted experiments in the use of compressed peat as locomotive fuel. From 1876 onwards locomotive practice was dominated by the unique presence of Bowman Malcolm who, appointed locomotive engineer at the tender age of 22, went on to serve until September 1922. Advocate of the Worsdell von Borries two-cylinder compound system, he embarked on a spell from 1890 to 1908 during which nothing but compound locomotives were produced. The first

NCC Locomotive Stocks (Standard Gauge)

Type	NCC(MR) 1903	NCC(LMSR) 1923 Class	No	NCC(BR) 1948 Class	No	Remarks
4–4–0	9	A	8			4 rebuilt to A1, 4 rebuilt to U2
		A1	5			One withdrawn 1947
		B	1			Rebuilt to B3, but withdrawn in 1947
		B1	2			Both rebuilt to B3 in 1932. Withdrawn 1946
		B3	2			Rebuilds from Class C 2–4–0s. Withdrawn by 1947
		D	1			Withdrawn 1944. Originally 2–4–0 Compound built 1895
		D1	1			Withdrawn 1946. Originally 2–4–0 Compound built 1895
		U	4			All rebuilt to Class U2
				A1	8	4 ex-Class A, 4 from 5 A1s built 1905–08
				U1	1	Rebuild from Class C1 2–4–0 Compound. Withdrawn 1949
				U2	18	4 ex-Class A, 4 ex-Class U, and 10 more built new in 1924/25
Totals (A)	9		24		27	
2–4–0	30	C	4		—	First BNCR 2–4–0 compounds. Built 1892/95
		C1	3		—	One rebuilt to Class U1 4–4–0
		F	2		—	2–4–0 Simples. Inside frames. Built 1880/85
		F1	1		—	2–4–0 Large boiler. Built 1880
		G	6		—	Double framed. Beyer & Sharp built, 1872/78
		G1	3		—	Double framed. Built by Sharp 1873/76
		H	4		—	Inherited from Belfast & Ballymena Railway
		I	2			Beyer-built for BNCR in 1868
Totals (B)	30		25		—	
0–6–0	16	E	2			Compounds, built by Beyer in 1892
		K	4			Long lived locomotives, with many rebuilds. Two were
		L	3			Belfast & Ballymena originals, built by Sharp in
		L1	2			1857. Remainder were contributed by Beyer & Sharp
				V	3	Superheated 0–6–0s supplied by Derby in 1923
Totals (C)	16		11		3	
0–4–2	2	M	1		—	Built by the BNCR in 1873. Withdrawn 1925
2–2–2	1				—	Relic of Ballymena, Ballymoney, Coleraine & Portrush Junc. Built 1855. Withdrawn 1906
2–4–0ST	4	J	4		—	Built as 2–4–0Ts 1883. Withdrawn 1932/34
0–4–0ST	2	N	2	N	1	One retained to 1951 to work Belfast Docks
0–6–0T	—	—	—	L	2	LMSR Fowler 3F 'Jinties', transferred to the NCC in 1944
2–6–0	—	—	—	W	15	Supplied by the LMSR, 1933–42
2–6–4T	—	—	—	WT	10	Supplied by LMSR, 1947. 8 more arrived during 1949/50
Totals (D)	9		7		28	
Grand totals A+B+C+D	64		67		58	(Standard gauge only)

Class U2 4–4–0 No 71 *Glenarm Castle* arrives at Magherafelt in July 1936. This line, forming an alternative route to the main line between Coleraine and Antrim via Ballymena, lost its passenger service in 1950 and was closed entirely in 1959. (*L&GRP*)

B&NCR compounds were seven Class C light 2–4–0s (1890–95), and two Beyer Peacock 0–6–0s followed in 1892. Thereafter, a brace of remarkable Class D heavy 2–4–0s, with 7ft 0in driving wheels, emerged from Beyer Peacock in 1895, five Class B locomotives introduced the 4–4–0 type in 1897/98, and a succession of 13 Class A heavy 4–4–0s bridged the years 1901 to 1908. A final four locomotives added before LMSR influence predominated were Class U simple 4–4–0s (1914 and 1922). The compound phase was over.

Just as in Britain Derby defeated Crewe in the early post-Grouping struggle for predominance, so Midland Railway influence did not fight shy of tackling the question of locomotive rationalisation in Northern Ireland. Von Borries compounding for instance evoked little sympathy, for the MR was already firmly committed to the Smith system. Considerable upheaval in NCC policy ensued, and the resultant programme of locomotive rebuilding, although destined to bring simplicity in the long run, is extremely difficult to follow. Perhaps it is more easily understood if one undertakes conjoint consideration of NCC locomotive stocks at three

distinct junctures in the company's equally complicated life.

In the three types most affected the pattern is clear. 4–4–0s were ultimately reduced to two standard classes, A1 and U2. Still based on the MRs Class 2 design, seven of the 10 U2s added in 1923/25 were built by North British Locomotive Company, Glasgow, and from this minority in numbers came the Class U2 nickname of 'Scotch engines'. Both A1s and U2s lasted well into the 1950s and No 74 *Dunluce Castle*, withdrawn in 1961, remains preserved in Belfast Museum. Where 2–4–0s were concerned, the last went in 1942, and by this time a positive miscellany of 0–6–0 classes had also been thinned. A final and comprehensive change of locomotive policy commenced in 1933, when the first of NCC's redoubtable 2–6–0s were introduced from Derby. All but two were named. Subsequently 18 2–6–4Ts, very similar to Fowler's 1927 LMSR design, which followed over the years 1947–50, more than sufficed to see the end of steam traction in Northern Ireland. Appropriately, No 4, last of the class, has been rescued from oblivion by the Railway Preservation Society of Ireland.

Above: Based on post-war LMS practice, 18 of these splendid 2–6–4 tanks were turned out at Derby for the NCC during the years 1946–50; visually they were a cross between the native British Fowler and Fairburn 2–6–4T types. They found full employment on the NCC, and handled everything from express passenger to goods traffic. (*T. Middlemass*)

Below: For shunting duties NCC acquired Sentinel 0–4–0 No 91 in 1925, together with a railcar from the same source. Both were withdrawn in 1932. (*T. Middlemass*)

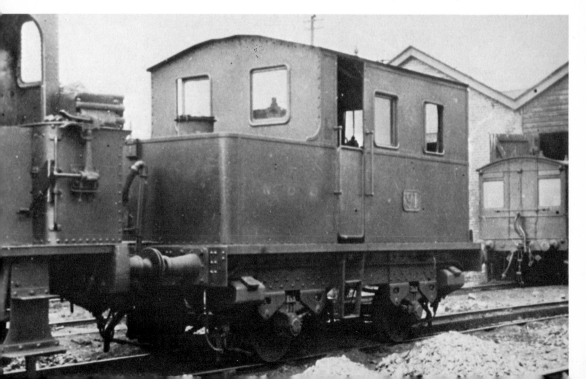

Above: In 1944, to meet increased wartime shunting requirements, two of the well-known LMS 'Jinty' tanks were transferred to NCC. No 19 (ex-LMS No 7553) is seen at York Road in August 1956. This locomotive, outliving the other, was withdrawn in 1963. (*J. L. Stevenson*)

Below: Larne Harbour station photographed in July 1936. Note the mixed gauge tracks where the 3ft gauge Ballymena & Larne line crosses or merges with the 5ft 3in gauge track. This results in complicated mixed gauge pointwork. By this time Larne had been resignalled with LMS upper quadrant seamaphore signals, the only station in Ireland to have them, lower quadrants remaining the standard type, except where somersault signals were used in parts of the north. Colour-light signals were, though, installed by the NCC from Belfast York Road to new junctions in the Greenisland and Monkstown area in the mid-1930s when the direct spur from Belfast towards Coleraine was built. (*L&GRP*)

Top: NCC first and third class composite coach, formerly the carriage portion of a steam rail motor. Two units were built soon after the turn of the century but the locomotive portions were scrapped just before the first world war and the coach portions rebuilt and used on ordinary Belfast local services thereafter. (*L&GRP*)

Above: LMS Derby-built brake tri-composite with first, second and third class for NCC services. These coaches were virtually identical in style with similar first/third brakes for the LMS in Britain, although some coaches were built to the wider 9ft 6in Irish loading gauge instead of the normal British 9ft. (*L&GRP*)

Below: The NCC was among early users of internal combustion vehicles in an endeavour to reduce costs. After a petrol railcar came diesel railcar No 2 seen here, a lightweight vehicle with integral construction and aluminium body built in 1934. The driving compartments seemed to be almost an after-thought, being raised above roof level so that the driver could see above the roofs of other vehicles if the railcar was in the middle or at the back of a train (driving trailer cars for diesel units had not been thought of by the NCC), although it did not really have the power to work with more than one trailer vehicle anyway. It was equipped with a pair of 125hp Leyland diesel engines. (*L&GRP*)

CHAPTER SIXTEEN
ULSTER TRANSPORT AUTHORITY
and
NORTHERN IRELAND RAILWAYS

UTA created by Act of Parliament: 1 October 1948
Replaced by Northern Ireland Railways Limited: 1 April 1968

No less reluctant than ever to focus on railways, even the Stormont Parliament was obliged in post-war years to take cognisance of Northern Ireland's rapidly worsening transport situation and a Bill passed in 1947 paved the way for amalgamation of all road and rail transport concerns whose activities were wholly contained within the Six Counties. The latter proviso, of course, automatically disqualified the GNR(I) from immediate inclusion in the scheme. None-the-less the NCC and B&CDR between them handed on a useful and compact railway network to the new authority. What transpired gave the lobby which constantly trumpeted the merits of road transport good reason to be satisfied. Despite initial optimism, the UTA's rail policy in the event proved so lacking in lustre that developments closely akin to Dr Beeching's activities across the Irish Sea resulted in wholesale closure of minor and branch lines. An inquiry held in 1952 in response to public unease brought little comfort. Generalities were politely exchanged, and the closures continued.

So adversely did the situation develop that when the GNR(I)'s northern assets passed into UTA ownership in October 1958 what might in normal

times have been a welcome doubling of UTA route mileage became a positive embarrassment. Things were helped little when the ex-GNR lines lost £$\frac{1}{4}$ million in the first year of UTA operation. By 1962 the UTA was on the verge of financial collapse. An inquiry was conducted, and subsequent government action, recognising that the experiment of integrating road and rail had failed, withdrew all road services from UTA's gift, and sanctioned further closures of ex-GNR lines, including the important one to Londonderry. As a further consequence what remained of Northern Ireland's railways were placed, on 1 April 1968, under the jurisdiction of a new company, the Northern Ireland Railways Ltd.

Mercifully this brought a marked improvement in railway thinking, though when dieselisation

Above: A former Great Northern diesel multiple-unit allocated to UTA approaches Annaghmore, near Portadown, in June 1964. UTA itself had acquired a variety of dmus itself, either new or by converting existing locomotive-hauled vehicles. Moreover UTA and NIR later preferred the more robust diesel-electric multiple-units for its new stock of the 1970s, built by British Rail Engineering with early BR MkII body style. (*J. L. Stevenson*)

Left: In 1974 Northern Ireland railways completed the reinstatement and modernisation of the former spur in Belfast between the GN line approaching Great Victoria Street at Central Junction and the Belfast & County Down line just outside Queens Quay terminus at Ballymacarrett Junction. As part of the modernisation a new station, Belfast Central, was constructed to replace both Great Victoria Street and Queens Quay and provide interchange between Bangor line trains and main line services to Dublin, also with Londonderry trains which were diverted from York Road terminus to run via Antrim and Lisburn into Belfast Central. The train is the 14.30 NIR Enterprise formed of the BR Mark IIB pattern stock built by British Rail Engineering about to leave for Dublin on 11 August 1980. (*Michael Baker*)

Right: Irish locomotive preservation is well exemplified by this shot of ex-GNR No 171 *Slieve Gullion* and NCC 2–6–4 tank No 4, taken at Rathpeacon on the Brian Boru railtour on 27 April 1969. (*J. L. Stevenson*)

Below: To work the NIR-based part of the Enterprise service NIR placed in service in 1970 three 1350hp diesel-electric Bo-Bos built by British Rail Engineering and Hunslet with English Electric equipment. Normally two are used, one at each end of an eight-car formation in multiple, although during lighter traffic periods one locomotive with a five-coach set operates push-pull fashion with control in one direction by a driving trailer coach. (*Michael Baker*)

came Eire's way the NIR was unable to match the CIE's main line diesel fleet, having previously switched entirely to railcar operation. Latterly, the NIR, clearly embarrassed at having to work the Belfast–Dublin 'Enterprise' express by railcar set, bought three diesel-electric locomotives from Doncaster in 1970 which, coupled to an eight-coach train specially built by Derby, and similar to BR's early MkII coaches, commenced push-pull operations. It is both touching and ironic that the NIR chose to name its three new diesels *Eagle*, *Falcon* and *Merlin*, after the GNR's fine, but comparatively short-lived, 4–4–0 compounds. By then, as far as Northern Ireland was concerned, only lines from Belfast to Londonderry, Portrush and Larne remained of the previous network. There has though been some development on NIR with the opening in the 1970s of the new Belfast Central station on the reactivated cross-city link between the GN and BCD lines, which replaced Queens Quay and Great Victoria Street stations. Moreover while the NCC York Road station still serves Larne trains, Londonderry services run from Central via Lisburn and the GN line to Antrim to regain the NCC Derry line.

Today, with a mileage less than half of the NCC after World War I, the NIR, like British Rail, continues to grapple with the stark economics of modern rail transport. Political events in Ireland do little to soften the agonies.

Locomotives
During the first 10 years of its chequered career the UTA acquired a very varied assortment of locomotives as shown in the table on page 96.

The fate of B&CDR locomotives has already been described. NCC locomotives worked on, but by 1960 practically only the Derby Moguls and 2–6–4Ts were left to handle the UTA's ever-decreasing needs. By 1965 the last of the Moguls had gone, and the tanks soldiered on for another half-decade as the UTA's last steam locomotives.

Where GNR locomotives were concerned, older types were withdrawn immediately the UTA acquired them, while those which survived were renumbered in 1960. Even then, again within five years, the last trace of working GNR(I) steam vanished. Fortunately three locomotive exhibits have been preserved, to remind us of days gone by.

Standard Gauge Locomotives Taken into UTA Stock

Type	From BCDR 1 Oct 1948	From NCC 1 Oct 1948	Added 1949/50	From GNR(1) 1 Oct 1958	Totals
2–6–0	—	15	—	—	15
4–4–0	—	27	—	28	55
2–4–0	1	—	—	—	1
0–6–0	4	3	—	38	45
0–4–2T	1	—	—	—	1
2–4–2T	3	—	—	—	3
2–6–4T	—	10	8	—	18
4–6–4T	4	—	—	—	4
4–4–2T	15	—	—	13	28
0–6–4T	1	—	—	4	5
0–6–0T	—	2	—	—	2
0–4–0ST	—	1	—	—	1
Totals	29	58	8	83	178
Diesels	2	4	—	28	34

UTA and NIR opted mainly for diesel multiple-units to replace steam, some power cars of which were originally multi-purpose cars for goods and parcels. Thus very few diesel locomotives have been required as shown in the centre table.

Two General Motors 2450hp diesel-electric Co-Cos, similar to CIE's 071 Class, have also been ordered, and were to be in use on Belfast–Dublin 'Enterprise' express trains early in 1981. Twelve additional BR Mk IIB coaches were transferred to NIR from BR's own stock, after being equipped with 5ft 3in gauge bogies.

NIR Railcars

UTA's railcar policy was pursued by NIR, but with more emphasis on diesel-electric types mostly built by British Rail Engineering and following BR Mk II designs. The units currently in stock are shown in the bottom table.

Diesel Locomotives in NIR Stock

Running Nos.	Wheel Arrangement	Built by	Date in service	HP	T/E lbs	No. of locos	Remarks
1–3	C	English Electric/ AEI	1969		25,000	3	Used for permanent way trains and shunting.
101–103	Bo–Bo	English Electric/ AEI/BR	1970	1350	42,000	3	For 'push-pull' working between Belfast and Dublin.
					Total	6	

Diesel multiple-units and railcars in NIR Stock

Running Nos.	Built by	Tons Weight	Date in service	
63–65	UTA/Rolls Royce	39½	1957	MOTOR COACHES
71–78	UTA/Eng. Elect.	62	1966	
67–69 81–99	BR/Eng. Elec./GEC	62	1974	
721–723 725–727 728	UTA/Eng. Elec.	29/30	1966	INTERMEDIATE TRAILERS
761–773	BREL, Derby	32	1974	
701–703 711–713 714	UTA/Eng. Elec.	30	1966	DRIVING TRAILERS
731–751	BR/Eng. Elec./GEC	35	1974	